Stay Encouraged

ENCOURAGING WORDS
AND LESSONS FOR PARENTS WITH EXCEPTIONAL CHILDREN

DIETRICH MCMILLAN

Published by:

EMPOWER ME BOOKS, INC.
A Subsidiary of Empower Me Enterprises, Inc.
P.O. Box 16153 Durham, North Carolina 27704
www.EmpowerMeBooks.com

ISBN: 978-1732773158

Printed in the United States of America

Stay Encouraged

ENCOURAGING WORDS
AND LESSONS FOR PARENTS WITH EXCEPTIONAL CHILDREN

I dedicate this book to every parent, caretaker, and every family member that has taken care of a loved one with extra needs. Remember, you are a special gift.

When we know who we are and whose we are, we can stand on a firm foundation that we are God's gift to this world. His masterpiece fearfully and wonderfully made.

~Dietrich

ACKNOWLEDGMENTS

First and foremost, I acknowledge and thank my God, Lord and Savior Jesus Christ, and the Holy Spirit. Without Him, this would not have been possible.

I honor and thank my Husband, Antoine, for his patience and support. I love you so much. For my inspirations, my son, Travis, and daughter, Brittney. I am so incredibly proud of you both. Continue to strive to be all that God will have you to be.

When God gifted me to you and you to me, He knew exactly what and who I needed. To my father and mother, Charles, and Deborah Dye, you both have taught me how-to walk-in integrity, remain faithful, and to love. I love you.

During one of the most challenging times in my life, you gave me words of encouragement that I will never forget, 'It's not your fault.' Those few words helped me get over a lot of hard days. Thank you for the talks and the encouragement, Delores McMillan, you are not just my mother in law, but my mother in love.

Thank you, Aunt Lucille McMillan. You will always be my Ram in the Bush. God sent you at the right time and moment that we needed you. Thank you for your heart of gold, not only for caring for our child but for all of the children in the family that you have taken in and cared for without complaint. God sees you, and He says, Well Done!

To my village, family, and friends, you have all been simply amazing and have embraced our family and differences. You have allowed us to enjoy life. You are all God sent.

Last but definitely not least, to my Pastor John C. Fitzpatrick., Jr., First Lady, Elder Pauline Fitzpatrick, and my OLCC Family– I love all of you. From the moment we stepped into the door, you took us just as we were and did not try to make us change to fit in. You have walked, played, talked to, run after, and embraced Brittney with open arms. You just let her be. Thank you.

ENCOURAGEMENT FOR THE PARENT OR CARETAKER:

Dear Beloved:

You are all that God has called you to be. Believe in your purpose and who you are even though your life may seem to be upside down, chaotic, and different. Still believe even when you feel that you are not capable, different, forgotten, unworthy and that you have lost. This book was designed for you to take time to reflect and build your confidence and love yourself. Know that God says, 'You Are'!

Even in the midst of heartache, doubt, chaos and uncertainty God's plan for you is to show you and to lift you up to His plan to prosper you. You have to choose how you look at who you are.

Every day you must proclaim, and you must remember that:

You Are like Jochebed and **YOU ARE CHOSEN**
You Are like the Shunamite Woman and **YOU ARE MORE THAN A CONQUEROR!**
You Are like Jonathan and **YOU ARE REMEMBERED!**
You Are like Esther and **YOU ARE PURPOSED!**
You Are like David and **YOU ARE VICTORIOUS!**
You Are like Mary Magdalene and **YOU ARE REDEEMED!**
You Are like Leah and **YOU ARE LOVED BY THE GREATEST!**

Your journey is your own. Do not ever forget to embrace it fully, learn from it and most importantly share it with others. Why? Because you are not alone. It is my desire that we all connect in some way to help encourage and build one another in our similarities, as well as our differences. Through the lessons your journey brings you, you will understand **WHAT IS YOUR FOCUS** and be able to see **THROUGH GOD'S EYES** because **JESUS KNOWS AND SEES** that **IT IS NOT YOUR FAULT.** So, **HAVE NO FEAR** and **DON'T GIVE UP!** God has provided a **RAM IN THE BUSH** so you can live life fully. So, do not be afraid, **SPEAK UP** and advocate for you, your child and family!!!!

I pray that you are able to ACKNOWLEDGE, BELIEVE AND CONQUER who you are and the lessons your journey brings. Remember that with Faith it is possible and through Jesus Christ you can do all things with His strength. I hope that you learn and know who you are and that you will embrace your journey. Last, I pray you will

Stay Encouraged!!!

Love,
Dietrich McMillan
Life is Designed by God

MY PRAYER FOR YOU

Dear Heavenly Father:

You are magnificent and wonderful. I thank You, and I am so grateful for the opportunity to tell the reader that they are all You have called them to be. I pray that every reader will acknowledge the love You have for them, and they believe that they are purposed and set apart for the great work ahead. I pray that through the doubts and difficulties, the reader will always come back to You, Lord and remember that through You, they are more than a conqueror and already have the victory.

Touch every reader and their family. Remind them often of who they are—direct their paths along their journey. Download your knowledge and wisdom. Give them the strength to remain faithful and to persevere through every challenge. Whisper in their ears daily of how You chose them, that You, Lord are with them, and they are not alone. Keep the reader uplifted and help them to

Stay Encouraged!!!

In Jesus' Name, I pray. Amen.

C O N T E N T S

DEDICATION
ACKNOWLEDGEMENTS
ENCOURAGEMENT LETTER
PRAYER

SECTION 1: YOU ARE

CONTENTS

OFFER OF SALVATION
ABOUT THE AUTHOR
BOOK REVIEWS

You Are...

Encouraging Words

You are an incredibly special person. God has created you to be a special gift. Your gift is unique and there will be times that you will not know what to do or where to go or what to say. I too have felt like this, but when I reflect on who I am and who God says I am, I have become more confident in knowing that I am a gift that God created and that my life, my journey is also a gift. These encouraging words are for you to remember who you are in God.

YOU ARE:

CHOSEN

REMEMBERED

LOVED BY THE GREATEST

MORE THAN A CONQUEROR

PURPOSED

REDEEMED

VICTORIOUS

These are only a few of the things God has said you are. So, I charge you to rise up and be the person that God has called you to be and to always

Stay Encouraged!

~Dietrich

1

CHOSEN

You are the Right One

SCRIPTURE: Exodus 2:1-10 (NIV)

"Now a man of the tribe of Levi married a Levite woman, ² and she became pregnant and gave birth to a son. When she saw that he was a fine child, she hid him for three months. ³ But when she could hide him no longer, she got a papyrus basket[a] for him and coated it with tar and pitch. Then she placed the child in it and put it among the reeds along the bank of the Nile. ⁴ His sister stood at a distance to see what would happen to him. ⁵ Then Pharaoh's daughter went down to the Nile to bathe, and her attendants were walking along the riverbank. She saw the basket among the reeds and sent her female slave to get it. ⁶ She opened it and saw the baby. He was crying, and she felt sorry for him. "This is one of the Hebrew babies," she said. ⁷ Then his sister asked Pharaoh's daughter, "Shall I go and get one of the Hebrew women to nurse the baby for you?" ⁸ "Yes, go," she answered. So the girl went and got the baby's mother. ⁹ Pharaoh's daughter said to her, "Take this baby and nurse him for me, and I will pay you." So the woman took the baby and nursed him. ¹⁰ When the child grew older, she took him to Pharaoh's daughter and he became her son. She named him Moses, saying, "I drew him out of the water."

Exodus 6:20 *Amram married his father's sister Jochebed, who bore him Aaron and Moses.*

SCRIPTURAL REVELATION: Many would read this particular scripture and say that Moses was the chosen one. Despite apparent self-esteem issues and speech impediment (see Exodus 6:30), Moses was chosen to fulfill God's purpose in delivering the Israelites from the Pharaoh. This conclusion is correct; however, I maintain that the true chosen one was his mother, Jochebed. Despite Pharaoh's orders to kill all newborn baby boys, she was chosen by God to birth the Israelite's deliverer. Jochebed was 130 yrs. old when she birthed Moses. Yes, Jochebed was older than Sarah when she had Isaac!!! God did it again. Considered to be a righteous woman, Jochebed proved God right by defying the Pharaoh's order to kill all baby boys. God gave Jochebed insight and wisdom that led to hiding her baby for three months, preparing a waterproof basket, and setting him in it among the water bank.

Imagine the difficulty of letting your child go, not knowing because of the pigmentation of his skin if he would be killed as ordered by Pharaoh. God certainly chose the right one. Not only did God choose Jochebed to birth Israel's deliverer. As an award of her faithfulness, after giving up her baby, Jochebed was chosen again to freely raise her very own son, while others were being slaughtered.

REVELATION: Have you ever wondered Why Me? I certainly did in the beginning. As I began to grow and learn, I started shifting my focus, and now my question is,

Why Not Me? I look back over my life, and I never did the ordinary. So, why wouldn't God trust something extraordinary to me? I have always had a knack in finding that silver lining in every cloud. This was confirmed to me when I had a conversation with my cousin, who also has children with exceptional needs. She told me that her husband said growing up, I always had a way of finding the good in everything. I did not realize I was that way when growing up. Even today, people ask how I do it and stay positive? Having a professional career as an attorney helping victims of domestic violence become victorious, a passion for serving others, husband, children, school, and still staying positive.

Yes, there are days I am overwhelmed, I am exhausted, but All I know is To God be the Glory. It is all Him, and He chose me to carry out His will and His purpose. I intend to do just that. I am confident that because He chose me, "that he who began a good work in you will carry it on to completion until the day of Christ Jesus." Philippians 1:6 (NIV)

MEDITATE AND ACTIVATE

ACKNOWLEDGE: You are Chosen. Chosen means one who is the object of choice or divine favor: an elect person (Miriam Webster). God knows you; He knows your strength, your weaknesses. He knows what you need and your capabilities. You have to know it for yourself. You are special, set above the rest. It is okay to humbly acknowledge that you have an extraordinary life.

Walk proud, chosen one!!!

1 Peter 1:15-16 But just as he who called you is holy, so be holy in all you do; for it is written: "Be holy, because I am holy."

BELIEVE: You are chosen. God has ordained You!!! You are ordained to be an extraordinary person. God is so amazing. When He has ordained a person to do a certain thing, that is precisely what happens despite it all. You possess a unique quality that not every person or parent has. Believe that

You are the Right One!!!

Ephesians 2:10 (KJV) For we are his workmanship, created in Christ Jesus unto good works, which God hath before ordained that we should walk in them.

CONQUER: Even when you do not have the strength when you are unsure of yourself, or you question why you – Always remember and go back to the sweet words of Jesus in

John 15:16 :

You did not choose me, but I chose you and appointed you so that you might go and bear fruit—fruit that will last—and so that whatever you ask in my name the Father will give you.

ENCOURAGING WORD:

When God has ordained you to do something great or be something great, it will not look ordinary. Just as God chose Jochebed to raise a deliverer, one who had self-esteem issues and a speech impediment. God has chosen you too. When you see how special you are to God, you will come to realize that not only do you have faith and trust in Him, but that also He has Faith and Trust in YOU.

PRAYER

Dear Heavenly Father, thank you for choosing me. Why you chose me, I will never know. Yet, I am honored and humbled that you loved me enough to trust me with your special gifts. I will walk in those things that you have ordained for me. I will do those things to the best of my abilities. I trust that because I am chosen that you will always be there and that I can stand on your Word that whatever I ask - wisdom, knowledge, peace, joy - in your name you will give to me. Thank you. In Jesus' Name,

Amen.

2

REMEMBERED I

You Are Not Forgotten

SCRIPTURE: 2 Samuel 9:1-7 (NIV)

David asked, "Is there anyone still left of the house of Saul to whom I can show kindness for Jonathan's sake?" ²Now there was a servant of Saul's household named Ziba. They summoned him to appear before David, and the king said to him, "Are you Ziba?" "At your service," he replied. ³The king asked, "Is there no one still alive from the house of Saul to whom I can show God's kindness?" Ziba answered the king, "There is still a son of Jonathan; he is lame in both feet." ⁴"Where is he?" the king asked. Ziba answered, "He is at the house of Makir son of Ammiel in Lo Debar." ⁵So King David had him brought from Lo Debar, from the house of Makir son of Ammiel. ⁶When Mephibosheth son of Jonathan, the son of Saul, came to David, he bowed down to pay him honor. David said, "Mephibosheth!" "At your service," he replied. ⁷"Don't be afraid," David said to him, "for I will surely show you kindness for the sake of your father Jonathan. I will restore to you all the land that belonged to your grandfather Saul, and you will always eat at my table."

SCRIPTURE REVELATION: David remembered the faithfulness of his dear friend Jonathon. Despite Jonathon's father Saul's attempt to kill David, David made sure he remembered the goodness of Jonathon. Jonathon recognized the anointing and was faithful to David as God's anointed king. Jonathon was loyal to David by helping him escape from Saul's wrath. God considered David a man after God's own heart. Remaining true to this anointing, David wanted to remember Jonathon. David learned that Jonathon had a loved one, a child that was injured as an infant and was permanently disabled. David made sure that Jonathon's legacy was well-taken care of. Just as God laid it on David's heart to remember Jonathon and his son, God will make sure you and your legacy are remembered.

REVELATION: It is easy to get lost in the day to day hustle of caring for others. Frequently it seems we are forgotten and that no one cares. Just as in the story of Jonathon, David could have forgotten about his friend. But David remembered Jonathon's goodness and faithfulness. People will not always understand why you care so much or even how you do it. I think of members in my family who cared for those ill and/or with special needs. I am reminded of my mom. I remember how my mom, who took care of my Great Aunt until her passing, going every week to the nursing facility to make sure she was being taken care of and getting her clothes to wash. Now, she is taking care of her elderly father with dementia. She and her sisters rotate faithfully, making sure he is loved and well taken care of. I also remember my mother in law, taking into her home several family members who were gravely ill and literally on their deathbeds. She wanted to make sure they were comfortable in their last days.

Last, I remember my Aunt in law coming to spend the summer with us. Not because we asked, but because she knew we needed help with our daughter. It was a total surprise, and we were so honored to have her with us for the summer.

I look back over these mighty women and the love they poured out to others. I pray that God will allow me to remember each of them each in a special way, For sure God will remember these caretakers and bless them mightily. I also believe that God will allow man to honor and bless them as well.

MEDITATE AND ACTIVATE

ACKNOWLEDGE: You are remembered. Acknowledge that you have a special place in God's heart. God will honor you for your faithfulness and your journey. You are not forgotten!!!

Isaiah 49:15-16 as God reminds His people that He has not forgotten them: "Can a mother forget the baby at her breast and have no compassion on the child she has borne? Though she may forget, I will not forget you! See, I have engraved you on the palms of my hands; your walls are ever before me."

BELIEVE: The good you do now will always be remembered.

The help you gave to others, even caring for the special gift God gave you, you will be remembered. That extra mile you went to make sure your loved one was taken care of, will be remembered. God remembers you; He will make sure that man remembers too. He will make sure that not only will you be remembered, but the thing that is closest to your heart will always be taken care of also. Just as David remembered Jonathon, God will remember you.

Hebrews 6:10 God is not unjust; he will not forget your work and the love you have shown him as you have helped his people and continue to help them.

CONQUER:

1. Do not get weary in well-doing. Caring for others with extra needs is hard, but we should still do good for them.

   Galatians 6:9-10 Let us not become weary in doing good, for at the proper time we will reap a harvest if we do not give up. Therefore, as we have opportunity, let us do good to all people, especially to those who belong to the family of believers.

2. Remain faithful and know that you will be rewarded and remembered.

   Matthew 25:34-40 speaks of a parable that Jesus spoke to his disciples about caring for others and what will happen. A parable is an earthly story with a spiritual meaning.

   [34] "Then the King will say to those on his right,

9

'Come, you who are blessed by my Father; take your inheritance, the kingdom prepared for you since the creation of the world. [35] For I was hungry and you gave me something to eat, I was thirsty and you gave me something to drink, I was a stranger and you invited me in, [36] I needed clothes and you clothed me, I was sick and you looked after me, I was in prison and you came to visit me.' [37] "Then the righteous will answer him, 'Lord, when did we see you hungry and feed you, or thirsty and give you something to drink?" [38] When did we see you a stranger and invite you in, or needing clothes and clothe you? [39] When did we see you sick or in prison and go to visit you? [40] "**The King will reply, 'Truly I tell you, whatever you did for one of the least of these brothers and sisters of mine, you did for me.'** [41] "Then he will say to those on his left, 'Depart from me, you who are cursed, into the eternal fire prepared for the devil and his angels. [42] For I was hungry and you gave me nothing to eat, I was thirsty and you gave me nothing to drink, [43] I was a stranger and you did not invite me in, I needed clothes and you did not clothe me, I was sick and in prison and you did not look after me.' [44] "They also will answer, 'Lord, when did we see you hungry or thirsty or a stranger or needing clothes or sick or in prison, and did not help you?' [45] "He will reply, 'Truly I tell you, whatever you did not do for one of the least of these, you did not do for me.' [46] "Then they will go away to eternal punishment, **but the righteous to eternal life."**
(emphasis added)

ENCOURAGING WORD:

God sees what you do and go through. He knows the care and faithfulness you exhibited to others. He will make sure that not only you are remembered, but that your loved one will be remembered too.

PRAYER

Dear Heavenly Father, sometimes I get so tired and weary. I at times, do not know whether I am coming or going. I even wonder if I can continue to do this. Thank you for your love and for remembering me. I rest in the comfort of your arms, knowing that you have not forgotten me, and you know my name. I praise you, Lord, and will remain faithful to you as I carry on your good works.

Amen.

3

LOVED

By the Greatest

SCRIPTURE: Genesis 29:31-35 (NIV)

"When the LORD saw that Leah was not loved, he enabled her to conceive, but Rachel remained childless. Leah became pregnant and gave birth to a son. She named him Reuben, or she said, "It is because the LORD has seen my misery. Surely my husband will love me now." She conceived again, and when she gave birth to a son she said, "Because the LORD heard that I am not loved, he gave me this one too." So she named him Simeon. Again she conceived, and when she gave birth to a son she said, "Now at last my husband will become attached to me, because I have borne him three sons." So he was named Levi. She conceived again, and when she gave birth to a son she said, "This time I will praise the LORD." So she named him Judah. Then she stopped having children."

SCRIPTURAL REVELATION: God had compassion and showed love to Leah due to the mistreatment from her family. She was not the prettiest girl on the farm, had a disfigurement (Genesis 29:17), and was down-right despised by her own husband, Jacob. Jacob used her to get to the love of his life - Rachel. Yet, Leah kept looking

12

for the love of her husband. Despite the lack of love from a man, God kept blessing Leah with sons. God blessed Leah's womb showing her who truly loved her. God. Finally, when her fourth son was born, Leah realized that she was loved by the Greatest. She named her son Judah-which means 'Give God Praise.' After Judah was born, for a moment, Leah stopped having children. God has a way of showing us His love. He will fulfill every gap, but we must recognize His ultimate love for us. We must give Him, not man, our attention and praise.

REFLECTION: Imagine how Leah must have felt always seeking the love of someone. It is a horrible feeling. Yet, because she had God's heart, she was blessed with the greatest gift of all. God blessed her so that it was through her we have the line of Judah, which bore the lineage of David and eventually our Savior, Jesus!!!!!! What can we learn from Leah? Take no thought of what others think about you. You are loved by the Greatest, and from His love, you are purposed; like Leah, you will birth greatness. Our lives may not be pretty, it may be difficult, but at the end of the day, God loves us.

Through our lives, others will see His light. It is through us that signs and wonders will prevail; that God gets the glory, and we will rest with Him one day. I do not know how Leah kept doing it, but I believe we have the same Spirit in us; we must always remember to give God the praise. We must turn our focus on Him when we feel unloved and out of sorts. He will then fulfill every gap. There were times

I felt worn out, left out, feeling like I am not good enough, not pretty, alone, and unloved. Then I look at my daughter, and she gives me the most beautiful smile. It is then I know the love of the Greatest. He has given me the most special being on this Earth, and He just reminded me through her smile that I am indeed loved by the GREATEST.

MEDITATE AND ACTIVATE

ACKNOWLEDGE: Know that God loves you. There is a saying that if He said it, then that settles it. You are loved, not only that, but you are loved by the greatest.

John 3:16 — "For God so loved the world (meaning you) that he gave his one and only son, that whoever believes in him shall not perish but have eternal life."

BELIEVE: You are beautiful inside and out. Believe that you are God's masterpiece - especially created for a special purpose determined long ago. An artist loves His created work.

Ephesians 2:10 (NLT) — "For we are God's masterpiece. . ."

Note: A masterpiece is a gem, jewel, treasure, perfection, prize, showpiece; this is how the Greatest artist sees you.

CONQUER:

1. Look in the mirror and see the beauty in you that God has created.

   Solomon 4:7 — "You are altogether beautiful, my darling; there is no flaw in you."

2. Know that God is not looking at your outward appearance, but your heart. He made you unique and your life special because He knows that your heart is good.

   1 Samuel 16:7 — "...The LORD does not look at the things people look at. People look at the outward appearance, but the LORD looks at the heart."

3. Seek and Praise God first in all you do, and you will be blessed.

   Matthew 6:33 — "But seek first his kingdom and his righteousness, and all these things will be given to you as well."

ENCOURAGING WORD:

Remain positive when you look and feel tired, when you do not feel pretty and feel no one understands. Take a moment to look at the special gift God has given to you and see the beauty. It is through that beauty you will know that you are blessed and loved by the Greatest.

PRAYER

Dear Heavenly Father, thank you for seeing me from the inside out. Thank you for seeing the beauty of my heart. When I am discounted and looked over by man, you see me, and you call me your masterpiece. I am the most blessed person because you, the Greatest, love me. I am Your work of art that will praise and glorify you all the days of my life. In Jesus Name,

Amen.

4

MORE THAN A CONQUEROR I

Crazy Faith!

SCRIPTURE: 2 Kings 4:8-37

⁸ One day Elisha went to Shunem. And a well-to-do woman was there, who urged him to stay for a meal. So whenever he came by, he stopped there to eat. ⁹ She said to her husband, "I know that this man who often comes our way is a holy man of God. ¹⁰ Let's make a small room on the roof and put in it a bed and a table, a chair and a lamp for him. Then he can stay there whenever he comes to us."
¹¹ One day when Elisha came, he went up to his room and lay down there. ¹² He said to his servant Gehazi, "Call the Shunammite." So he called her, and she stood before him. ¹³ Elisha said to him, "Tell her, 'You have gone to all this trouble for us. Now what can be done for you? Can we speak on your behalf to the king or the commander of the army?" ¹⁴ "She replied, "I have a home among my own people." "What can be done for her?" Elisha asked. Gehazi said, "She has no son, and her husband is old." ¹⁵ Then Elisha said, "Call her." So he called her, and she stood in the door- way. ¹⁶ "About this time next year," Elisha said, "you will hold a son in your arms." "No, my lord!" she objected. "Please, man of God, don't mislead your servant!"

servant!" ¹⁷ But the woman became pregnant, and the next year about that same time she gave birth to a son, just as Elisha had told her. ¹⁸ The child grew, and one day he went out to his father, who was with the reapers. ¹⁹ He said to his father, "My head! My head!" His father told a servant, "Carry him to his mother." ²⁰ After the servant had lifted him up and carried him to his mother, the boy sat on her lap until noon, and then he died. ²¹ She went up and laid him on the bed of the man of God, then shut the door and went out. ²² She called her husband and said, "Please send me one of the servants and a donkey so I can go to the man of God quickly and return." ²³ "Why go to him today?" he asked. "It's not the New Moon or the Sabbath." "That's all right," she said. ²⁴ She saddled the donkey and said to her servant, "Lead on; don't slow down for me unless I tell you." ²⁵ So she set out and came to the man of God at Mount Carmel. When he saw her in the distance, the man of God said to his servant Gehazi, "Look! There's the Shunammite! ²⁶ Run to meet her and ask her, 'Are you alright? Is your husband all right? Is your child all right?'" "Everything is alright," she said. ²⁷ When she reached the man of God at the mountain, she took hold of his feet. Gehazi came over to push her away, but the man of God said, "Leave her alone! She is in bitter distress, but the LORD has hidden it from me and has not told me why." ²⁸ "Did I ask you for a son, my lord?" she said. "Didn't I tell you, 'Don't raise my hopes'?" ²⁹ Elisha said to Gehazi, "Tuck your cloak into your belt, take my staff in your hand and run. Don't greet anyone you meet, and if anyone greets you, do not answer. Lay my staff on the boy's face." ³⁰ But the child's mother said, "As surely as the LORD lives and as you live, I will not leave you." So he got up and followed her. ³¹ Gehazi went on ahead and laid the staff on the boy's face, but there was no sound or response. So Gehazi went back to meet Elisha and told him, "The boy has not awakened."

^{32} *When Elisha reached the house, there was the boy lying dead on his couch.* ^{33} *He went in, shut the door on the two of them and prayed to the LORD.* ^{34} *Then he got on the bed and lay on the boy, mouth to mouth, eyes to eyes, hands to hands. As he stretched himself out on him, the boy's body grew warm.* ^{35} *Elisha turned away and walked back and forth in the room and then got on the bed and stretched out on him once more. The boy sneezed seven times and opened his eyes.* ^{36} *Elisha summoned Gehazi and said, "Call the Shunamite." And he did. When she came, he said, "Take your son."* ^{37} *She came in, fell at his feet and bowed to the ground. Then she took her son and went out."*

SCRIPTURAL REVELATION: There are so many lessons we can glean from this mighty woman. God's prophet promised the Shunamite woman a child. It seemed the child might have perhaps suffered from what we call today migraines or maybe some other brain disorder causing significant headaches. The child died after complaining about his head. Upon the child passing away in her arms, the Shunamite woman mustered up enough strength within her to not dwell in the circumstance of her promised child was dead, but that she was going to do all she could to overcome anything standing in her way to get help. She had 'crazy faith' to believe that if she could get to the man of God, he could help her bring her son back to life. All she knew was that this Prophet through God so far delivered on every promise he made to her. To get to the prophet, the Shunamite woman had to get through four obstacles.

Obstacle 1: Tradition: doing things the same way.
In 2 Kings 4:22-25, the Shunamite woman asked her

husband to allow her to take a donkey and   servants to go to the Prophet, Elisha. Her husband's response was not to go today because of the tradition of only going to the Prophets during certain seasons or times as custom required. The Shunammite woman's response to her husband was that everything is alright. She then took the donkey and, servants, and set off to find the prophet, Elisha. She did not let the fact that it was not a particular season or day stop her. She had a mission, and she was aiming to conquer what she set out to do.

Obstacle 2: Others holding you back, caring about what others think.

2 Kings 4:27. When the Shunammite woman reached the man of God, his servant tried to stop her by pushing her away. However, Elisha rebuked his servant. God will never push you away.

Obstacle 3: When the professionals do not know

2 Kings 4:27 Elisha explains his rebuke of the servant. Elisha, the prophet, does not know why the Shunamite woman is in such distress. Even when man does not know, Gd does and will reveal what needs to be done at the appointed time.

Obstacle 4: When nothing seems to work

2 Kings 4:31. Elisha's servant, Gehazi, tried to revive the Shunammite woman's son. He failed.

Despite her son dying in her arms and the emotions she was going through, the Shunamite woman overlooked everything to get to God. She more than conquered all of these things, and through her faith, her son regained life.

REFLECTION: I often get crazy looks when I begin to speak about what others think is impossible or just out of the ordinary. I got crazy eyes when I started collecting boxes to pack up my home. People asked me when the moving date was. I would tell the person, I do not know, but I need to start packing our belongings. Oh, the looks. We did not have anywhere to move to at the time, but I believed that if God said it, that settles it. So, I started packing. Within 30 days, we were qualified to purchase a home and had found the house we wanted. God tested my faith during that time. On the eve of our closing around 5 pm, our loan officer called and said we needed to bring to the table $3,000, or we would not be able to close. I called my husband and told him what she said.

We did not have $100 to our name at that time. We thought everything was paid for and going to be paid for at the closing. Yet, the program that gave us the best deal said we needed to show we could afford the loan. The crazy part of this program was that we would get the $3,000 back after a couple of weeks. Crazy right? Of course, my heart and mind were set on moving into this house.

My husband said, 'Well, I guess that's it; we will not be able to do it.' I said, "The devil is a liar." I prayed and asked God for some help and what to do. I wanted my toddler son and my baby girl to have a house of their own, with individual rooms. God dropped three people in my spirit. I called my mom, a good friend of mine and my husband's mother. I asked each of them if they could help us with the money, and we would pay it back as soon as we got it back from the closing. They all said YES!!!! I called my husband and told him we got the money. Then called the loan officer around 7 pm and told her we got the money; we will be closing tomorrow. She was stunned.

I still apply this same crazy faith to my life today. Despite research and studies, I have faith in our daughter. I will have conversations in which she will clearly speak with me clearly and concisely – she is adding to her vocabulary of 'I love you' with 'bye-bye' and some babbling ending with bye-bye when she is ready to go for a ride or outside. Our daughter has stunned the communication pathologist by clearly saying, 'I Love You.' The pathologist, amazed, noted that these words were difficult for someone with little to no speech. My response: 'To God be the Glory. She will speak. It is in her.'

Like the Shunamite woman:
1) I refuse to let what seems to be the ordinary, traditional way of doing things stop me from going forward. Some would say wait until you get approved for the loan before packing. No! Exhibit faith and pack now.

2) Your looks do not phase me. You can't stop me. I will declare my faith and belief in Jesus and what He tells me. Look crazy all you want. If He said it, that settles it.

3) Even when the professionals - i.e., loan officers, therapists do not know - I will keep holding on to the belief and professing my faith.

4) I will not ascribe to what looks like a failure to dictate my confidence that my God can do anything. If one thing does not work, I will find another way that is in the will of God. Why? Because Jesus has given me the power, and I am more than a conqueror!!!!!

MEDITATE AND ACTIVATE

ACKNOWLEDGE: There will always be obstacles, but with crazy faith, one can overcome all. It may take some work or some time, but you will overcome it.

Romans 8:37 No, in all these things we are more than conquerors through him who loved us.

BELIEVE: If you keep your faith and stand on His Word, whatever you face, you will be more than a conqueror.

I John 5:4 For whatever is born of God overcomes the world. And this is the victory that has overcome the world — our faith.

CONQUER: What are your obstacles? Just because what we see seems one way, does not necessarily have to be. God has given us excellent stewardship over the things of this Earth, including our loved ones. However, the Shunamite woman was seemingly barren (as she did not have a son). That was her first obstacle, yet God gave her a child. As stated before, there are many lessons we can glean from this story. We can also learn from this woman on being More Than a Conqueror if we:

1. <u>KEEP AND HAVE CRAZY FAITH:</u> Do not ever give up. Keep believing. It is through your belief/faith that you will be able to conquer the impossible.

    Mark 9:23 (NKJV) *Jesus said to him, "If you can believe, all things are possible to him who believes."*

2. <u>KEEP OUR 'EYES ON THE PRIZE.'</u> Stay the course and stay focused, keep Jesus first, and you will be able to conquer more than what is set before you.

    Philippians 3:15-16 (MSG) *So let's keep focused on that goal, those of us who want everything God has for us. If any of you have something else in mind, something less than total commitment, God will clear your blurred vision—you'll see it yet! Now that we're on the right track let's stay on it.*

3. DO NOT LET OBSTACLES OR
   DISTRACTIONS STOP YOU.
   Run with perseverance and whatever is in your
   way, refer back to number 2 and keep your
   eyes on Jesus.

   *Hebrews 12:1-2(a) Therefore, since we are
   surrounded by such a great cloud of
   witnesses, let us throw off everything that
   hinders and the sin that so easily entangles.
   And let us run with perseverance the race
   marked out for us, fixing our eyes on Jesus, the
   pioneer and perfecter of faith.*

ENCOURAGING WORD:

We must remember that we must not look at our present circumstance, or what we see before us. As children of God, we must exercise what we call 'crazy faith' even the more with the extra challenges we have been graciously blessed to bare. We must have faith just like the Shunamite woman. You are more than a conqueror - Keep your eyes on the prize and have crazy faith.

PRAYER

Dear Heavenly Father, we are eye gazers. What we see is what we believe. Today God, I ask you to increase my belief, increase my faith, and not look at what I see, not look at my circumstances but to look to you. I know with faith through you, all things are possible. You are the perfecter, and my focus will remain on you and not my circumstances. In Jesus' Name, Amen.

5

MORE THAN A CONQUEROR II

Yes You Can!

SCRIPTURE: Joshua 1:6-9

⁶ Be strong and courageous, because you will lead these people to inherit the land I swore to their ancestors to give them. ⁷ "Be strong and very courageous. Be careful to obey all the law my servant Moses gave you; do not turn from it to the right or to the left, that you may be successful wherever you go. ⁸ Keep this Book of the Law always on your lips; meditate on it day and night, so that you may be careful to do everything written in it. Then you will be prosperous and successful. ⁹ Have I not commanded you? Be strong and courageous. Do not be afraid; do not be discouraged, for the LORD your God will be with you wherever you go. "

SCRIPTURAL REVELATION: Joshua was Moses' servant that God chose to continue and fulfill the promises given to Moses. Joshua conquered the promised land by defeating mighty armies, giants, and every occupant that did not belong there. Can you imagine the Israelites wandering for 40 years and, not having to come against those that are strong and have lived in this land of milk and honey?

Yet, they, when obedient to God's command and word, defeated every foe. God knew the state of mind, the physical agility of the Israelites and He continuously told the new leader 'be strong and courageous' or 'Do not be afraid or discouraged.' Sometimes when we have not had our proper rest, we do not know what is next or how to defeat the giant; we can become fearful, terrified, and sometimes downright petrified at the unknown. Joshua, now being a leader, probably felt the same as he saw these giants, mighty armies and kingdom in the land God promised to the Israelites. Despite what Joshua saw before him, he kept his faith in God and went forward. Although he didn't execute a perfect plan, as you can see in a few of the chapters in Joshua; however, he still more than conquered the land in which God promised and divided it among the 12 sons (tribes) of Israel.

REFLECTION: When I first read the book of Joshua, I kept wondering why God kept telling him to be strong, courageous, and not to be afraid. I soon realized that God knows the obstacles, circumstances, and dilemmas you face and will face. God understands that things may seem too much and can be scary. Such as when an individual facing the loss of a loved one now alone or the loss of a home rendering an individual homeless. How about when you go into labor two months early, and you are two states away. You had everything prepared, your baby was born pre-maturely outside of the comforts of your home. Later it was communicated that your child has to stay in the hospital while you are released. Your baby is having difficulty breathing and maintaining her oxygen levels. Day by day, you do not know what the outcome is going to be. Scary right?

I am sure so many can relate. All of this happened to us. All I can remember is believing and having faith in God. I traveled back and forth from Georgia to North Carolina every week. Giving a mandate to my mother-in-love to make sure she visited her granddaughter every day while I was gone from Thursday to Sunday to finish my course work. I would return on Sunday and see our daughter every day until she was released (thankfully she was released early). I did not have to make the choice to leave her, yet my faith was stronger than any feelings I had at that time. I was petrified, had so many thoughts running through my head, couldn't concentrate, I was exhausted, yet I found the strength through Jesus, and I knew that I had to continue and trust that God would take care of her. Honestly, I did not think I was going to make it; I just knew I had to rest on the promises of God. Not just for me, but for her, for my family, and because God said I can and must.

MEDITATE AND ACTIVATE

ACKNOWLEDGE: Just like Joshua, you can conquer whatever you face. No matter how tired, disappointed, or big that thing is in front of you, you can conquer it. God promised in the Old Testament to be right there with Joshua, and today he promises that 'You can do all things through Christ who strengthens you.' Philippians 4:13 Paul reiterates the promise of God in the New Testament. Understand that with this acknowledgment, the journey or task may not be comfortable. It can be challenging, frustrating, seemingly disappointing, and you may even want to give up, but you must remember you can do it with the help of Jesus. He promises to be there.

John 16:33 "I have told you these things, so that in me you may have peace. In this world you will have trouble. But take heart! I have over- come the world."

BELIEVE: Philippians 4:13 is a scripture often quoted but is it believed. Do we as parents draw on the strength of Jesus? Think about it; the scripture does not have a period after 'I can do all things.' Yet, this is the very thing we try to do 'All things.' We multitask, we make sure everyone else is squared away, and at the end of the day, we have no umph, no strength, often feeling defeated when circumstances come out differently than we thought. Why is that? Is it because we need the second half of that scripture, 'through Jesus who strengthens me.' Even Paul, in II Cor 12:9-10, stated that in his weaknesses, he is made strong through Jesus. Many would even say that Paul had a disability or something that debilitated him i.e. 'thorn in his side' (II Cor 12:7). Yet, he drew on the strength and grace of God to overcome and conquer whatever was set before him. What Paul exhibited was belief, no matter his circumstances.

II Corinthians 12:9-10 But he said to me, "My grace is sufficient for you, for my power is made perfect in weakness." Therefore I will boast all the more gladly about my weaknesses, so that Christ's power may rest on me. That is why, for Christ's sake, I delight in weaknesses, in insults, in hardships, in persecutions, in difficulties. For when I am weak, then I am strong.

CONQUER: God gave Joshua instructions on how to be
MORE THAN A CONQUEROR:

1. OBEY THE WORD. "Be careful to obey all the law my servant Moses gave you;(v7) God understands that we are human, which is why he says be careful!!! If a mistake happens, repent and ask for forgiveness. Do not let it stop you from conquering the things of God.

James 1:25 *But whoever looks intently into the perfect law that gives freedom, and continues in it—not forgetting what they have heard, but doing it—they will be blessed in what they do.*

2. STAND FIRM ON THE WORD. ". . .do not turn from it to the right or to the left, that you may be successful wherever you go." (v.7) You must remain focused on the word and the promises of God. Be steadfast, immovable, stand on His Word.

I Corinthians 15:58 (NKJV) *Therefore, my beloved brethren, be steadfast, immovable, always abounding in the work of the Lord, knowing that your labor is not in vain in the Lord.*

3. ALWAYS REMEMBER THE WORD OF GOD. "Keep this Book of the Law always on your lips;"(v9) By remembering God's Word and having it in your heart will help you keep and stand firm His Words as you continue on your path towards conquering those things God has for you.

Psalms 119:11 I have hidden your word in my heart that

I might not sin against you.

4. MEDITATE ON THE WORD EVERYDAY. "...
meditate on it day and night, so that you may be
careful to do everything written in it. Then you will
be prosperous and successful." (v9) Remember
God's Word and pray and meditate on it every day.

Psalms 1:1-3 (KJV) *Blessed is the man who walks not
in the counsel of the ungodly, Nor stands in the path of
sinners, Nor sits in the seat of the scornful; But his
delight is in the law of the Lord, And in His law he
meditates day and night. He shall be like a tree Planted
by the rivers of water, That brings forth its fruit in its
season, Whose leaf also shall not wither; And whatever
he does shall prosper.*

5. DO NOT FEAR GOD IS WITH YOU! "Do not be
afraid; do not be discouraged, for the LORD your
God will be with you wherever you go." The
journey may seem long and arduous but keep the
faith and remember that God is with you wherever
you are.

6.

Hebrews 13:5-6 - *"... because God has said,
"Never will I leave you; never will I forsake
you."[from Deuteronomy 31:6]* [6] *So we say with
confidence, "The Lord is my helper; I will not be
afraid. What can mere mortals do to me?"*

ENCOURAGING WORD:

Stop looking at your circumstances, feeling defeated, or scared. Stand on the Word of God, pray, seek His wisdom and knowledge by meditating on His Word, and be confident knowing that God is with you. God is not just with you, but He is in you. Remember, that with Jesus, YOU are More than a Conqueror, Yes You Can!

1 John 4:4 You, dear children, are from God and have overcome them, because the one who is in you is greater than the one who is in the world.

PRAYER

Dear Heavenly, I can and will do whatever is set before me. I will do it bravely and with the knowledge that you are with me. Please, Lord, continue to, and I believe that you will strengthen me in my moments of fear, doubt, despair, grief, or anything that is not of your Spirit. I know full well that you have not given me the Spirit of Fear, but of Love, POWER, and a sound mind. With you, nothing can come against me and prosper. Thank you, Lord, for your grace and mercy. I will be careful to obey, remember, and meditate on your word. When I do these things, I know I can do ALL things through you because you strengthen me, and I AM MORE THAN A CONQUEROR. In Jesus' name, Amen.

6

PURPOSED

For Such a Time as This

SCRIPTURE: Esther 4:12-14

*"When Esther's words were reported to Mordecai, he sent back this answer: "Do not think that because you are in the king's house you alone of all the Jews will escape. For if you remain silent at this time, relief and deliverance for the Jews will arise from another place, but you and your father's family will perish. **And who knows but that you have come to your royal position for such a time as this?"***

SCRIPTURAL REVELATION: Esther is a young lady that is an orphan. Her uncle Mordecai raised her after her parents' death. Esther was raised during a time in which the Israelites were held in captivity by the Babylonians. On top of losing her parents, she also lived a life as a Jew enslaved by the Babylonians. Esther had to hide her heritage, knowing that she too could be killed at any moment if it was found out who she was. Yet, despite her background, heritage, and being enslaved, Esther receives favor from man and God. Esther probably never believed that she would become a Queen of a Babylonian Empire, especially during a time when Jews were hated and mistreated. Having no mother and father indeed could have been a significant loss adding to layers of doubt. Yet, that loss could have helped propel her to her purpose or destiny as Queen. Every detail in the Bible has some significance. What was the significance of Esther having no parents and having to be raised by her uncle Mordecai? Maybe if she had her parents, at least one of them, Esther would not have been free (or they would not have encouraged her) to become a part of the king's harem. They would have discouraged her because of her ethnicity. With some encouragement, Esther seemed to have readily followed the instructions of her uncle. Her faith and obedience saved an entire nation.

God's excellent design in his purpose allowed Esther to find favor with the King and save the Jewish people from death. I encourage you to read Esther, in particular, the second chapter. Look closely at how God's hand works when it comes to fulfilling purpose. God knew before He allowed the Jews to be held in captivity, knowing that there would come a time for His people to be delivered. God placed Esther, as well as Mordecai, in such a position at an appointed time to save His people.

What you will also notice in this book, which has been controversial for some scholars, is that it does not mention God anywhere. Yet, you see God's purpose being fulfilled. So, what does this say? We should remember that even when we feel like God is not there, in our plight, in our loss, in our despair, we should always remain grateful, gracious, faithful, and hopeful. That even in the midst of it all, in due time, our purpose will prevail, and that God's purpose will be fulfilled.

REFLECTION: In my early days, I wish I could have been more like Esther and never asked, Why me? Why was I chosen to lead this life? Why do I often feel forgotten, less than, feeling that I have lost the battle? It took a long time, but I eventually realized that through it all, God's hand is in everything. Whatever His purpose is, it will be fulfilled, and it will be fulfilled through me. My journey did not begin when my daughter was born; it started when I was born. I look back over my life and can see God's hand in my growing up although not fully understanding then who He is, but knowing He is there. I sometimes have that ah-ha moment, and I say, 'OK, God, that's why I went through that particular trauma or issue.' Every detail, everything works according to the good of God. *"And we know that in all things God works for the good of those who love him, who have been called according to his purpose." Romans 8:28*
Esther's past helped push her into the destiny that God orchestrated for her. Her journey created freedom that she would not have otherwise had to help and save others.

Like Esther, I learned that my journey is not for me. sharing, I can help others navigate, learn who they are, and uplift them. I look back and remember times having conversations with friends that have children with extra needs. I was able to give an account of my life and how my husband and I overcame difficult issues—for instance, talking with a parent who was frustrated with her 6-year-old child with autism not sleeping through the night. We had a great conversation about the lack of sleep we both have because, quite frankly, it seems our children do not require much sleep. A 15-minute nap appears to give them enough energy for another 24 hours. Yet, we know that the lack of sleep comes frustration and aggression. She was experiencing everything we experienced. I began sharing how I handle my daughter's sleep issues and provided tips on how the parent could manage her own emotions and frustrations because the child picks up on it. The next morning, I received a text stating after following my suggestion she and her child had a good night's sleep.

MEDITATE AND ACTIVATE

ACKNOWLEDGE: God's plan is a mystery. He will not reveal everything to you at once, but he knows your appointed time for your purpose to be fulfilled. Know that you have a purpose, and it will come to fruition.

Jeremiah 29:11 - " For I know the plans I have for you," declares the LORD, "plans to prosper you and not to harm you, plans to give you hope and a future."

BELIEVE: You must know that God's purpose for you is great even when you do not see Him and understand how you will achieve or get through your journey; believe that your steps are ordered, and know that at the right time, your purpose will be fulfilled.

Psalms 37:23 - "The steps of a good man are ordered by the LORD, And He delights in his way."

CONQUER:

1. Like, Esther, accept the challenge that God has given to you. You may not know the result, but your purpose will be fulfilled. Do not ask why me? But accept - Why not me?

   II Peter 1:10-11(MSG) - *"So, friends, confirm God's invitation to you, his choice of you. Don't put it off; do it now. Do this, and you'll have your life on a firm footing, the streets paved and the way wide open into the eternal kingdom of our Master and Savior, Jesus Christ."*

2. When you have accepted God's plans for you, then allow Him to use you according to His purpose.

   Ephesians 2:10 - "For we are God's handiwork, created in Christ Jesus to do good works, which God prepared in advance for us to do."

3. Use your journey to speak life to yourself and others.

   I Thessalonians 5:11 - "Therefore encourage one another and build each other up, just as you are doing."

ENCOURAGING WORD:

God knows His plans for you. Trusting His plan is perhaps the hardest thing to do when your world seems always to be chaotic. But when we look at those that have gone before us, we see through faith that His plan never fails, and His purpose is fulfilled in DUE TIME and the right season.

There is a time for everything, and a season for every activity under the heavens:
a time to be born and a time to die, a time to plant and a time to uproot, a time to kill and a time to heal,
a time to tear down and a time to build, a time to weep and a time to laugh,
a time to mourn and a time to dance,
a time to scatter stones and a time to gather them,
a time to embrace and a time to refrain from embracing, a time to search and a time to give up,
a time to keep and a time to throw away, a time to tear and a time to mend,
a time to be silent and a time to speak, a time to love and a time to hate,
a time for war and a time for peace.
ECCLESIASTES 3 : 1 - 8

PRAYER

Dear Heavenly Father, thank you for the life you
have given.
Thank you for every detail of life, whether it was
good, threatening, or ugly. It may not have been
understood then, but the experience is given; the
steps taken have all been embraced. This journey
given will be used to uplift, motivate, and
encourage others. Thank you for your love, trust,
and PURPOSE for such a time as this.
Amen.

7

YOU ARE

Redeemed!

SCRIPTURE: Luke 8:1-2

After this, Jesus traveled about from one town and village to another, proclaiming the good news of the kingdom of God. The Twelve were with him, ²and also some women who had been cured of evil spirits and diseases: Mary (called Magdalene) from whom seven demons had come out;

SCRIPTURAL REVELATION: Redeemed means in Hebrew 'ga'al' meaning to deliver, redeem, act as a kinsman, avenge. The basic use of this word had to do with the deliverance of people or things that have been sold for debt. Jesus redeemed Mary Magdelene. Mary was possessed by seven demons. It is not precisely known what the demons were, but we know that somehow, somewhere throughout the time, she was enslaved to the enemy.

However, when she met Jesus, He bought her back unto Him and delivered her from her possession. He saw all that she was going through and how the enemy wronged her by possessing her. Yet, Jesus loved her so much that he delivered her. He redeemed her. We see that throughout Mary's life, she followed Jesus. Mary is referred to as one of Jesus' disciples.

Often being listed first (except when recorded with the mother and aunt of Jesus) shows that she was highly respected. Can you imagine as a disciple telling others about the goodness and love of Jesus along with the powerful testimony of how Jesus delivered her from seven demons. Mary Magdelene, despite her past, not only was she loved by Jesus, she was chosen to be the carrier and deliverer of the greatest news ever. She was the first to proclaim - that our Lord has indeed been resurrected and He Lives!!!! (Mark 16:9-10)

REFLECTION: Living with regret of doing something you know you should not have done is the worst. You will find yourself always trying to make up for it; it causes you to second guess yourself, and worst of all, it separates you from the love of God. I learned that I would make mistakes, but I cannot dwell in them. God asks that we come to him with a repentant heart and change our ways. This is why David was considered a man after God's own heart. It was not because David was handsome or perfect that he killed Goliath, but because he was a murderer, adulterer, womanizer, and he was even disobedient to God's specific instructions. Yet, each time he realized his mistake, he sincerely repented and worshipped God!!!! I did not do all of those things, but there are some things I wished I had not done in my youth. Unfortunately, I cannot change the past. However, I can certainly advocate for those that may be walking down the same path. Hopefully, I can keep them from making the same mistakes by telling my story and showing how God redeemed and delivered me from my demons just as he saved and delivered Mary Magdalene.

MEDITATE AND ACTIVATE

ACKNOWLEDGE: That there is nothing that can separate you from the love of Christ. He loves you, and He will redeem, deliver, bring you back unto Him just as he saved this woman with SEVEN demons. He will redeem you too.

Romans 8:38-39 For I am convinced that neither death nor life, neither angels nor demons, neither the present nor the future, nor any powers, neither height nor depth, nor anything else in all creation, will be able to separate us from the love of God that is in Christ Jesus our Lord.

BELIEVE: That you are worthy of redemption and that God will take care of you and save you from your enemies or the enemy. In Lamentations 3:58, the writer, thought to be Jeremiah the prophet, gives hope in a time when the children of Israel had lost all hope. The children of Israel had lost all hope due to the conditions that they were living in as captives of the Babylonians. Jeremiah reminded the Israelites that no matter what you have done, God will take up your case and redeem (deliver) you.

Lamentations 3:58-59 You, Lord, took up my case; you redeemed my life. LORD, you have seen the wrong done to me. Uphold my cause!

CONQUER:
1. Understand that Jesus loves you, despite it all.
   Romans 5:8 *But God demonstrates his own love for us in this: While we were still sinners, Christ died for us.*

2. We should always give thanks to the Lord for he is good, and his love endures forever. Read Psalms 107 (included after the Encouraging Word) and see that no matter where you are in life, God loves you, and He will always draw you back to Him.

3. I love the way the Message version says Do not let anything, the enemy, or past mistakes separate you from the love of God.

Romans 8:31-39 (MSG) So, what do you think? With God on our side like this, how can we lose? If God didn't hesitate to put everything on the line for us, embracing our condition and exposing himself to the worst by sending his own Son, is there anything else he wouldn't gladly and freely do for us? And who would dare tangle with God by messing with one of God's chosen? Who would dare even to point a finger? The One who died for us—who was raised to life for us!—is in the presence of God at this very moment sticking up for us. Do you think anyone is going to be able to drive a wedge between us and Christ's love for us? There is no way! Not trouble, not hard times, not hatred, not hunger, not homelessness, not bullying threats, not backstabbing, not even the worst sins listed in Scripture: They kill us in cold blood because they hate you. We're sitting ducks; they pick us off one by one. None of this fazes us because Jesus loves us. I'm absolutely convinced that nothing—nothing living or dead, angelic or demonic, today or tomorrow, high or low, thinkable or unthinkable— absolutely nothing can get between us and God's love because of the way that Jesus our Master has embraced us.

ENCOURAGING WORD:

The entire Word of God expresses His love or you. He has redeemed you time and time again because He loves you.

"Fear not, for I have redeemed you; I have summoned you by name; you are mine. When you pass through the waters, I will be with you, and when you pass through the rivers, they will not sweep over you. When you walk through the fire, you will not be burned; the flames will not set you ablaze. Since you are precious and honored in my sight because I love you," and know that "I have swept away your offenses like a cloud, your sins like the morning mist. Return to me for I have redeemed you." With Love, Lord
(Isaiah 43:1-2,4; 44:22)

PSALMS 107
Message Version
1-3 Oh, thank God—he's so good!
His love never runs out.
All of you set free by God, tell the world!
Tell how he freed you from oppression,
Then rounded you up from all over the place,
from the four winds, from the seven seas.

4-9
Some of you wandered for years in the
desert,
looking but not finding a good place to live,
Half-starved and parched with thirst,
staggering and stumbling, on the brink of
exhaustion.
Then, in your desperate condition, you called
out to God.
He got you out in the nick of time;
He put your feet on a wonderful road
that took you straight to a good place to live.
So thank God for his marvelous love,
for his miracle mercy to the children he loves.
He poured great draughts of water down
parched throats; the starved and hungry got
plenty to eat.

10-16
Some of you were locked in a dark cell,
cruelly confined behind bars,
Punished for defying God's Word,
for turning your back on the High God's
counsel—
A hard sentence, and your hearts so heavy,
and not a soul in sight to help.

Then you called out to God in your
desperate condition; he got you out in the
nick of time.
He led you out of your dark, dark cell, broke
open the jail and led you out. So

thank God for his marvelous love,
for his miracle mercy to the children he loves; He
shattered the heavy jailhouse doors,
he snapped the prison bars like matchsticks!

17-22

Some of you were sick because you'd lived a bad life,
your bodies feeling the effects of your sin; You couldn't
stand the sight of food,
so miserable you thought you'd be better off dead.
Then you called out to God in your desperate condition;

he got you out in the nick of time.
He spoke the word that healed you,
that pulled you back from the brink of death.
So thank God for his marvelous love,
for his miracle mercy to the children he loves;

Offer thanksgiving sacrifices,
tell the world what he's done—sing it out!

23-32
Some of you set sail in big ships;
you put to sea to do business in faraway ports.
Out at sea you saw God in action,
saw his breathtaking ways with the ocean:
With a word he called up the wind—
an ocean storm, towering waves!
You shot high in the sky, then the bottom dropped out;
your hearts were stuck in your throats.
You were spun like a top, you reeled like a drunk,
you didn't know which end was up.
Then you called out to God in your desperate

condition;
he got you out in the nick of time.
He quieted the wind down to a whisper,
put a muzzle on all the big waves.
And you were so glad when the storm died down,
and he led you safely back to harbor.
So thank God for his marvelous love,
for his miracle mercy to the children he loves.
Lift high your praises when the people assemble,
shout Hallelujah when the elders meet!
33-41

God turned rivers into wasteland,
springs of water into sunbaked mud;
Luscious orchards became alkali flats
because of the evil of the people who lived there.
Then he changed wasteland into fresh pools of water,
arid earth into springs of water,
Brought in the hungry and settled them there;
they moved in—what a great place to live!
They sowed the fields, they planted vineyards,
they reaped a bountiful harvest.
He blessed them and they prospered greatly;
their herds of cattle never decreased.
But abuse and evil and trouble declined
as he heaped scorn on princes and sent them away.
He gave the poor a safe place to live,
treated their clans like well-cared-for sheep.

42-43
Good people see this and are glad;
bad people are speechless, stopped in their tracks.
If you are really wise, you'll think this over—
it's time you appreciated God's deep love.

PRAYER

Dear Heavenly Father, thank you for your love.
Thank you for forgiving me of my sins. Thank
you for delivering me from demons and those
things that are not of you. Thank you for being a
good, good father that may chastise me out of
love, but is always there to also comfort and guide
me. I praise you forever and know that you loved
me so much that you will never give up on me. I
am redeemed, and I say so!
In Jesus' Name, Amen.

8

VICTORIOUS

You Win!

SCRIPTURE: *1 Samuel 17:38-50*

[38] "Then Saul dressed David in his own tunic. He put a coat of armor on him and a bronze helmet on his head. [39] David fastened on his sword over the tunic and tried walking around, because he was not used to them. "I cannot go in these," he said to Saul, "because I am not used to them." So he took them off. [40] Then he took his staff in his hand, chose five smooth stones from the stream, put them in the pouch of his shep- herd's bag and, with his sling in his hand, approached the Philistine. [41] Meanwhile, the Philistine, with his shield bearer in front of him, kept coming closer to David. [42] He looked David over and saw that he was little more than a boy, glowing with health and handsome, and he despised him. [43] He said to David, "Am I a dog, that you come at me with sticks?" And the Philistine cursed David by his gods. [44] "Come here," he said, "and I'll give your flesh to the birds and the wild animals!" [45] David said to the Philistine, "You come against me with sword and spear and javelin, but I come against you in the name of the LORD Almighty, the God of the armies of Israel, whom you have defied. [46] This day the LORD will

deliver you into my hands, and I'll strike you down and cut off your head. This very day I will give the carcasses of the Philistine army to the birds and the wild animals, and the whole world will know that there is a God in Israel. [47] All those gathered here will know that it is not by sword or spear that the LORD saves; for the battle is the LORD's, and he will give all of you into our hands." [48] As the Philistine moved closer to attack him, David ran quickly toward the battle line to meet him. [49] Reaching into his bag and taking out a stone, he slung it and struck the Philistine on the forehead. The stone sank into his forehead, and he fell facedown on the ground. [50] So David triumphed over the Philistine with a sling and a stone; without a sword in his hand he struck down the Philistine and killed him."

SCRIPTURAL REVELATION: Many know the story of David and Goliath, of how a young shepherd boy used a slingshot and a stone to take down a giant. David is a shepherd, and because of his age, he would have typically been thought of as naïve, incompetent, or uneducated. He used a slingshot and stone - child's play, right? What this story shows is that you do not need a lot to be victorious. All you need is faith in God and through Him, use whatever you have. Whatever you have will be enough.

REFLECTION: Having faith in God and knowing He will guide you through is sometimes all you need. At times it may seem like it cannot be done. We feel like the Israelite army in the early part of 1 Samuel 17, believing they were already defeated, afraid to make a move to go against the giants. I can remember feeling defeated. I felt like a failure; time after time, door after door was closed, shut in my face. I was questioning if I was a good parent. Did I do all I could do? I have even told God; I cannot do this. Raising our daughter is too hard; I am not good at it. I learned over the years when I feel like this is not to take for granted the 'small' things that I have done - the slingshots and stones. I emphasize 'small' because, in the grand scheme of things, nothing is ever too small for God to get the glory and victory. Not only that, we should be just like David when he used something unconventional. David refused Saul's armor; it simply was not for David or his style. David instead used what was comfortable for him and what he was an expert at his faith in God and the slingshot and stone.

The Giant: When our daughter was born two months early, two states away from her home, the doctors and nurses said babies born prematurely have difficulty attaching and making eye contact. Of course, we could not accept what the doctors/nurses were saying (just as David did not accept the notion that Goliath could not be defeated)

The slingshot and stone: Our expertise - all we knew was that we loved our daughter. So my husband and I made sure that every day, all day long, our daughter heard the words 'I Love You' and not only she heard it, but we made her look in our face and make eye contact when we said it. Now she says I love you and make sure you see and hear her.

The Victory: The speech therapist coming to me and saying - 'I am amazed that your daughter can say 'I Love You' despite her lack of speech. Those are hard words to say.' Yes, even though she is deemed not to have speech - she says, 'I LOVE YOU' and will look at you when you say it. The simple act of saying it to her every day with eye contact helped her develop this. (Note: At the time of this writing, we, my daughter and I, have some great

Conversations - I do not understand what she is saying, but she will make sure I am looking at her when she is babbling, and yes, I respond as if I know what she is saying. Why? Because delayed is not denied, and WE ARE VICTORIOUS in all things through Jesus Christ.)

MEDITATE AND ACTIVATE

ACKNOWLEDGE: Jesus is with you, you have already won. It does not matter what it looks like; it does not matter how you feel; it does not matter who says no or comes against you; you have already won. Give God thanks anyway.

I Cor 15:57 (NIV) But thanks be to God! He gives us the victory through our Lord Jesus Christ.

BELIEVE: In everything, Jesus has won it all for you. Have faith that you are doing what you can for you and your child. Nothing you do to build yourself and your family is too small. It is the little things that take down the giants. You are doing what needs to be done, that you are accomplished, and victory is yours. You Win!!!

I John 5:4 *For every child of God defeats this evil world, and we achieve this victory through our faith.*

CONQUER:
1. Have faith and recognize that you are already victorious if God is with you, who or what can be against you.

Deuteronomy 20:4 For the Lord your God is the one

who goes with you to fight for you against your enemies to give you victory.

Romans 8:31 . . .If God is for us, who can be against us?

2. Whatever giant you face, speak victory over it. You have the power.

Proverbs 18:21 (KJV) Death and life are in the power of the tongue

Get a victory song in your Spirit. Whenever you doubt yourself sing that song. Praise God through it all and come out the other side as the Victor you already are. When I took the bar exam to become an attorney, I began doubting and thinking crazy thoughts. I asked the proctor if I could go to the bathroom. I went to the bathroom and started singing 'Victory is Mine' until every doubt was erased, and I felt confident again. Yes, I was victorious and passed the bar the first time. Even now, I need to encourage myself and sing this song to remember that Victory is mine, Victory is mine, Victory today is mine. I told Satan, get thee behind. Victory today is mine.' (Writers: Alvin Darling/Dorothy Norwood)

Psalm 96:1-2 Sing a new song to the Lord! Let the whole earth sing to the Lord! Sing to the Lord; praise his name. Each day proclaim the good news that he saves.

ENCOURAGING WORD: Don't be so quick to overlook the small things. What you may see as little are significant accomplishments, and that makes you victorious. YOU WIN!!!!

PRAYER

Dear Heavenly Father. I declare and decree in Jesus' name that every giant in my life is defeated. I, through Jesus, am victorious, and victory today is mine. With You Lord with me, there is nothing I cannot bring down. You are for me, so who can be against me. That means I WIN. In Jesus' name, Amen.

9

REMEMBERED II

Your Request Are Not Forgotten!

SCRIPTURE: Luke 8:40-56,

[40] *Now when Jesus returned, a crowd welcomed him, for they were all expecting him.* [41] *Then a man named Jairus, a synagogue leader, came and fell at Jesus' feet, pleading with him to come to his house* [42] *because his only daughter, a girl of about twelve, was dying. As Jesus was on his way, the crowds almost crushed him.* [43] *And a woman was there who had been subject to bleeding for twelve years,* [c] *but no one could heal her.* [44] *She came up behind him and touched the edge of his cloak, and immediately her bleeding stopped.* [45] "Who touched me?" Jesus asked. *When they all denied it, Peter said, "Master, the people are crowding and pressing against you."* [6] *But Jesus said, "Someone touched me; I know that power has gone out from me."* [47] *Then the woman, seeing that she could not go unnoticed, came trembling and fell at his feet. In the presence of all the people, she told why she had touched him and how she had been instantly healed.* [48] *Then he said to her, "Daughter, your faith has healed*

you. Go in peace." [49] *While Jesus was still speaking, someone came from the house of Jairus, the synagogue leader. "Your daughter is dead," he said. "Don't bother the teacher anymore."* [50] *Hearing this, Jesus said to Jairus, "Don't be afraid; just believe, and she will be healed."* [51] *When he arrived at the house of Jairus, he did not let anyone go in with him except Peter, John and James, and the child's father and mother.* [52] *Meanwhile, all the people were wailing and mourning for her. "Stop wailing," Jesus said. "She is not dead, but asleep."* [53] *They laughed at him, knowing that she was dead.* [54] *But he took her by the hand and said, "My child, get up!"* [55] *Her spirit returned, and at once she stood up. Then Jesus told them to give her something to eat.* [56] *Her parents were astonished, but he ordered them not to tell anyone what had happened."*

SCRIPTURAL REVELATION: There is a lot in this scripture concerning the woman with the issue of blood and the resurrection or healing of Jairus' daughter. For this purpose, the focus I want to turn your attention to is that no matter what is going on, Jesus will not forget you or your request. It is impossible - He is God!!!! Jairus came to Jesus with a request to help his daughter. Jesus was on his way to see Jairus' daughter, but then, a woman came and seemingly distracted Jesus from going to the house of Jairus. As Jesus was speaking to the woman, news came that Jairus' daughter was dead. The person delivering the information tells Jairus to forget about Jesus coming now; it is too late. Hearing this, Jesus tells Jarius not to worry, believe that she is just sleep. Jesus goes to Jairus' home, and a crowd of people making a bunch of commotion is there, and Jesus kicks them out. Before long, Jarius' daughter is standing up. Request fulfilled.

REFLECTION: How many times the situation looks bleak, and you have prayed and cried, prayed and cried, but it seems that it would not be fulfilled. Others seem to get their breakthrough – like the woman with the issue of blood, but you do not. You wonder what about me, God? Remember me? I am your servant too. I have been faithful. I believe. Did you forget me?

I have felt like this many times. Even now, I have to refocus myself to not look at others getting their well-deserved breakthrough or blessing. Sometimes, I want to throw in the towel. I cannot count the times I did give up and threw in the towel, only for God to throw it back at me and say, wipe your tears, I am not done yet. He always sends me that glimmer of hope to let me know He sees me, He heard my request, and I am not forgotten. The first time I took our daughter to church, she was so fussy. She cried and cried and cried; I could not get her to stop. I was so frustrated. My son was sitting beside me like he had ants in his pants and she was crying. Church had not started yet, so I asked God to let her stop crying before the service began. I did not think he heard my prayers and was about to leave.

Just as I had given up, here comes this lady. I was still relatively new at the church, so she introduced herself to me and asked to hold my daughter. I figured why not and gave Brittney to her. Well, would you know my daughter stopped crying? She sat down next to me, and my daughter remained quiet. I was in awe. Oh my God, my prayers were answered. Maybe not how I thought, but He remembered my request and sent some help. Besides, little did I know at the time, but this lady was a home daycare provider and agreed to enroll Brittney into her daycare.

Just as Jairus, you may be at your wits' end. You may want to give up, throw in the towel, say nevermind. Yet, at the right moment, when you think it is not going to happen, Jesus says: 'Don't worry. Do not be afraid. Just Believe.' Perhaps, like Jairus, you are expecting a breakthrough or your prayers to be answered in a certain way or at a particular time. However, you must remember that God heard your request. He has not forgotten your request. He will answer your request at the appointed time. Not only that, did you see what Jesus did for Jairus?

He not only healed his daughter but brought her back to life! Just like He did for me, Jesus not only answered my prayer but gave me a daycare provider to help care for our daughter. Won't He Do It?!

MEDITATE AND ACTIVATE

ACKNOWLEDGE: God remembers you. He hears your prayers. They may not be answered when and how you expect, but He will answer them. Even if it seems to take a while, God has not forgotten. He is not a man. He cannot forget. Read other scriptures in which God remembered prayers and not only remembered but gave much more than expected:

Luke 1:11-17 *Then an angel of the Lord appeared to him, standing at the right side of the altar of incense. [12] When Zechariah saw him, he was startled and was gripped with fear. [13] But the angel said to him: "Do not be afraid, Zechariah; your prayer has been heard. Your wife Elizabeth will bear you a son, and you are to call him John. [14] He will be a joy and delight to you, and many will rejoice because of his birth, [15] for he will be great in the sight of the Lord. He is never to take wine or other fermented drink, and he will be filled with the Holy Spirit even before he is born. [16] He will bring back many of the people of Israel to the Lord their God. [17] And he will go on before the Lord, in the spirit and power of Elijah, to turn the hearts of the parents to their children and the disobedient to the wisdom of the righteous—to make ready a people prepared for the Lord."*

2 Kings 20:1-6 *In those days Hezekiah became ill and was at the point of death. The prophet Isaiah son of Amoz went to him and said, "This is what the LORD says: Put your house in order, because you are going to die; you will not recover." [2] Hezekiah turned his face to the wall and prayed to the LORD, [3] "Remember, LORD, how I have walked before you faithfully and with wholehearted devotion and have done what is good in your eyes." And Hezekiah wept bitterly. [4] Before Isaiah had left the middle court, the word of the LORD came to him: [5] "Go back and tell Hezekiah, the ruler of my people, 'This is what the LORD, the God of your father David, says: I have heard your prayer and seen your tears; I will heal you. On the third day from now you will go up to the temple of the LORD. [6] I will add fifteen years to your life. And I will deliver you and this city from the hand of the king of Assyria. I will defend this city for my sake and for the sake of my servant David.'"*

BELIEVE: You are important to God. Your request is important to God. If God remembers a small bird like a sparrow, He remembers you, the one He breathed life into.

Luke 12:6-7 *Are not five sparrows sold for two pennies? Yet not one of them is forgotten by God. Indeed, the very hairs of your head are all numbered. Do not be afraid; you are worth more than many sparrows.*

CONQUER: Feeling forgotten is not an easy thing to overcome. Sometimes there are more questions than answers. But, when you make your request known to God, know that He hears you, and it will not be forgotten. Also, understand that it will require:

Patience and Waiting: Not every request will be immediately fulfilled. We have to trust God and his timing and wait on him.

II Peter 3:8-9 *But do not forget this one thing, dear friends: With the Lord, a day is like a thousand years, and a thousand years are like a day. The Lord is not slow in keeping his promise, as some understand slowness.*

Do not become discouraged: Can you see Jairus pacing back and forth, waiting for Jesus to finish talking to this woman who took Jesus' attention? Jesus was on a mission to save Jairus' daughter, and now He is talking to some woman, and by the way, it was illegal for her to be in the crowd and touch someone.

Remember that God heard you, and your prayers will be answered too. The greatest gift you can give someone is to Rejoice when they receive their blessing. Just like you, they may have had to wait.

Romans 12:15 *Rejoice with those who rejoice; mourn with those who mourn.*

Keeping the faith: Hold firm to the Word that God heard you and your prayer will be answered.

Mark 11:24 *Therefore I tell you, whatever you ask for in prayer, believe that you have received it, and it will be yours.*

ENCOURAGING WORD:

Just because it seems to be taking a while, always remember that delayed does not mean denied.

PRAYER

Dear Heavenly Father. You know what is best and the appointed time to answer my prayer. Thank you for so graciously loving me. I know that you remember me, and you have heard my request. Sometimes, the wait gets hard, but I know in the appointed time, my request will be answered, and I will patiently and faithfully wait to receive it as promised. In Jesus' name.
Amen

Encouraging Words

These lessons were mostly written about three years ago. When I began writing these lessons, I had no clue that it would actually be a part of a book. I simply wrote them to remind and encourage myself as we continue on our journey with our daughter. Writing these helped me get through the emotional difficulties of feeling guilty, feeling like we were out here with no help and always questioning am I doing what is right. I learned to always talk to God about whatever I am going through and ask for His wisdom and His knowledge on how to handle every difficulty. What I discovered is that God is always there and when I seek Him and give it to Him, I can better appreciate His joy, His peace, and the love our daughter has to give.

I pray these lessons encourages you as you find your way to finding peace, joy, love and understanding. These are reflective of my journey, yours may be different, yet there is one thing we all must do,

Stay Encouraged!

Life is a journey and everyday there is a lesson. Some days the lessons will be hard, some days they will be easy. Learn and appreciate every day and every lesson while on your journey. When you are at the end of the journey, you will have the pleasure of looking back and seeing that it was all worthwhile.

~ Dietrich

10

<u>YOU GOT THIS</u>

What's Your Focus?

SCRIPTURE: 1 Peter 1:15 -16 (MSG)

As obedient children, let yourselves be pulled into a way of life shaped by God's life, a life energetic and blazing with holiness. God said, "**I am holy; you be holy.**"

SCRIPTURAL REVELATION: Peter writes this message to the Jews and Gentiles as an instruction on how to live. Due to the persecution and ostracization of the Christians who were the minority in Rome, Peter reminded and encouraged the believers to live their lives set apart from the non-believers. Despite the sin around them, focus on the living God and the Holiness in them.

To be holy refers to a state of being set apart from defilement. The Hebrew word translates "holy" as a term meaning "separate." Thus, what is holy is separated from common use, or held sacred, especially by virtue of it being clean and pure.

Paul in Romans 12:2 (NIV) even speaks about being set apart and not conforming to this world as he encourages the Roman Christians - *'Do not conform to the pattern of this world, but be transformed by the renewing of your mind. Then you will be able to test and approve what God's will is—his good, pleasing and perfect will.'*

REFLECTION: As I look back over my life, I have always felt I was different; never really fit in with the in crowd. Never really wanted to, especially after seeing some of the things other people were doing. Yet, I just realized how being different and set apart really factors into my life now. What I realized a while ago is that this world belongs to my daughter and I will no longer try to make her conform to the ideas and ways of this world. I no longer stress on whether she should sit down in church and/or be quiet. If she sits, great, she gets acknowledgment and accolades for it. However, if she is on the move due to sensory overload, then let's go somewhere and move (normally if this is the case one of the mothers of the church will come get her before I have a chance to move.)

Sitting in church one day, this couple comes in with a beautiful little girl. Their daughter was very vibrant, 4/5-year-old. The parents wanted her to be in the service with them, to sit still and not talk out loud. This was difficult for the little girl. We finally encouraged the parents to let one of our ministers take her upstairs or outside. It was not that she was a problem, but for any 4/5-year-old, sitting still and being quiet is a pleasant challenge and to add autism on top of that is even more challenging. The little girl sat still as long as she could (I thought she did excellent) but after having her senses heightened with praise and worship, calming down would require some time and effort. I tried to explain to the parents that rather than forcing her to conform to what we would do, allow her to do what she can and then let her burn off the energy. Unfortunately, the parents were adamant about making the child conform to their idea of what is normal, rather than letting the child be a child and be herself. They ended up leaving church early that day out of frustration.

I must admit, I used to think the same way and stopped everything because my child could not conform. Now that I know better and understand that my child is different and set apart for the glory of God, I find alternatives that complement her. I focus on her strengths, not whether she is conforming to the standards that are set. These also include those standards set by professionals based on her diagnosis.

MEDITATE AND ACTIVATE

ACKNOWLEDGE:

1. That God has given you a special stewardship that is different than others and the mainstream.

   Psalm 24:1 *The earth is the Lord's, and everything in it, the world, and all who live in it;*

2. That God has chosen you to be separate and holy, because He knows your strength and who you are that is not ordinary, but extraordinary.

   Ephesians 1:4 *For he chose us in him before the creation of the world to be holy and blameless in his sight.*

BELIEVE:

1. You are set apart or separated from common use, your life is sacred to God and you should believe that you are different in the things of God.

   Galatians 1:15-16 (NLT) *But even before I was born, God chose me and called me by his marvelous grace. Then it pleased him to reveal his Son to me so that I would proclaim the Good News about Jesus to the Gentiles.*

2. Your assignment as a steward over your exceptional child's life is sacred and should not be defiled by thinking it is a burden.

Psalm 127:3 *Children are a gift from the Lord; they are a reward from him.*

CONQUER:

1. Do not force conformity. Remember our children are set apart and our lives are set apart for a particular purpose. It was not meant to conform to the world's ideas or thinking of how we should be.

2. Embrace the difference and do not focus so much on it but focus on how to make the world conform to what you and your child need.

3. Advocate for your child, not for conformity. Advocate even when they try to put your child on a certain track because this is what most kids with that diagnosis do. Know your child. Refuse to focus on conforming to the set standards, allow your child to set the standard.

Always remember: Romans 12:2 *Do not conform to the pattern of this world but be transformed by the renewing of your mind. Then you will be able to test and approve what God's will is—his good, pleasing, and perfect will.*

ENCOURAGING WORD:

As parents with special ability kids the greatest thing we want is for our children to be included and not excluded. We can become so focused on trying to make our kids a part of the 'ordinary' world like 'normal' kids that we overlook the most beautiful thing about them. Their 'extraordinariness', their differences. God says you are holy because I am holy. Holy means to be set apart from the world. Our children are holy. They are set apart because of their purity as well as their differences and challenges. Even more so, we as parents have been set apart on a special assignment/mission to care for these sensitive souls. To speak to them. Not change them, but to embrace their very beings. So rather than trying to make them fit into the world, let them make their own way and set the standards. After all, shouldn't that be what we teach all of our children?

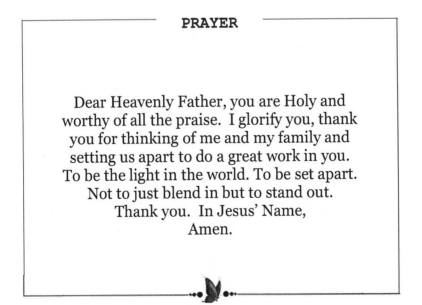

PRAYER

Dear Heavenly Father, you are Holy and worthy of all the praise. I glorify you, thank you for thinking of me and my family and setting us apart to do a great work in you. To be the light in the world. To be set apart. Not to just blend in but to stand out. Thank you. In Jesus' Name, Amen.

11

Through Gods' Eyes

SCRIPTURE: I Samuel 16:7
But the Lord said to Samuel, "Do not consider his appearance or his height for I have rejected him. The Lord does not look or judge a thing in the same manner as a man. Man looks at the outward appearance, but the Lord looks at the heart.

SCRIPTURAL REVELATION: 1 Sam 16:1-3 - When God sought to replace King Saul with a new king, He told Samuel to go to the house of Jesse to anoint the new king. When Samuel arrived, he saw handsome young men that <u>looked</u> to be the ideal figure of a king. As Samuel went to each of these young men, God told Samuel that these men were not the chosen king. Thus, telling Samuel that He looks at the heart of man. Eventually, David was brought in from shepherding his sheep and was anointed over his brothers.

REFLECTION: It was not until I asked God to open my eyes, to give me wisdom and clarification to handle my daughter's meltdowns when things begin to change. I prayed to God to help me understand. He then showed me that He had her in His hands and that He was waiting for me to see her beauty.

Of course, I have always loved my daughter, and I knew that she was exceptionally made. But it was not until after years of frustration, lack of understanding, and tears that I finally asked God to show me her. It was then that life took on a whole new meaning and things began to change - instead of not wanting to go into the church - I now at times can't get her to leave; instead of worrying if she is going to have a meltdown in the store or restaurant, she will now walk through the store or sit with very little problem.

Just as Samuel was told to stop looking at the natural and look through [God's eyes], at the unseen, the heart (which is hidden and protected), I too had to learn to look through the lens of God. That is where I found my king, the true jewel of my daughter.

We must always remember that our children are a heritage of the Lord, and the fruit of the womb is His reward. (Psalms 127:3).

MEDITATE AND ACTIVATE

ACKNOWLEDGE: Accepting our children for who they are, what they look like, and how they act is the first step into learning them, ourselves, and God's plan. Sometimes we only see what is in front of us rather than what God sees! Once we get past the surface, we can begin to deal with the underlying issues effectively. We must understand that there is a purpose in everything!

Hebrews 13:2 Reminds us n*ot to forget to entertain strangers, for by doing so, some people have entertained angels without knowing it.*

Luke 12:22-24 *Do not worry about food or your outward appearance, look at the ravens, you are worth far more than they.* Jesus tells his disciples to stop looking at life circumstances, but if the birds and fields are cared for, so shall you. You are worth more than the birds and fields.

When looking through the eyes of God, you will understand that:

1. He sees our children, and they are perfect in his eyes; accepting what God sees is far better than what man sees. Remember, His thoughts are higher than our thoughts! He goes much deeper and looks at the heart.

2. Circumstances are much more than what they look like; praise Him anyway and let God take care of the rest.

BELIEVE:

1. God's eyes are not tainted; despite what it looks like, your child has a purpose in God. God knows who we are and who our children are.

Psalms 139:13-16 (MSG) *Oh yes, you shaped me first inside, then out; you formed me in my mother's womb. I thank you, High God— you're breathtaking! Body and soul, I am marvelously made! I worship in adoration— what a creation! You know me inside and out, you know every bone in my body; You know exactly how I was made, bit by bit, how I was sculpted from nothing into something. Like an open book, you watched me grow from conception to birth; all the stages of my life were spread out before you, The days of my life all prepared before I'd even lived one day.*

2. God knows and has a plan for everyone.

Jeremiah 29:11, *"For I know the plans I have for you," declares the Lord, "plans to prosper you and not to harm you, plans to give you hope and a future.*

CONQUER: So, how do I begin to see what God sees?
1. Pray – ask God to help you see things as he sees them?

Elisha in 2 Kings 6:17 *And Elisha prayed, "Open his eyes, Lord, so that he may see." Then the Lord opened the servant's eyes, and he looked and saw the hills full of horses and chariots of fire all around Elisha.* This request was to show Elisha's servant that God is protecting them from the Syrian Army. The servant had become afraid of what he saw before him – the Syrian Army. However, when God opened his eyes, he could see that God had encamped his angels (horses and chariots) around Elisha.

2. Do not be afraid of what you see before you; ask God to open your eyes to see beyond your circumstance.

Psalm 119:18 (message) Ask God to *open my eyes so I can see what you show me of your miracle-wonders.*

3. Keep your focus on God.

Psalm 121:1-2 *I will lift up my eyes to the hills—From whence comes my help? My help comes from the Lord, who made heaven and earth.*

Matthew 6:33 *But seek first his kingdom and his righteousness, and all these things will be given to you as well.*

4. Begin to change the way you think or see your circumstance – rather than look at it as an obstacle, look at it as an opportunity – to learn, understand and grow with your child.

Ephesians 4:22-2 *You were taught, with regard to your former way of life, to put off your old self, which is being corrupted by its deceitful desires; to be made new in the attitude of your minds; and to put on the new self, created to be like God in true righteousness and holiness.*

5. In all things, Give God Glory!

I Corinthians 10:31 *So whether you eat or drink or **whatever you do**, do it all for the glory of God.*

ENCOURAGING WORD:

God's eyes have perfect vision. When you use his lenses, you will not need glasses or contacts because you will then see what He sees - A Masterpiece.

Ephesians 2:10 *For we are God's masterpiece.*

PRAYER

Dear Heavenly Father.
You created me, you designed my family, and I thank you for it all. Thank you for making each one of us unique. Thank you for loving each of us as we are. God, I choose to look at my life and my family's life through your lenses. What perfect vision and beauty you created. I am so forever grateful for the artwork you have created.
In Jesus' name,
Amen.

12

SPEAK UP: ADVOCATE

What is Your Rebuttal?

SCRIPTURE: Matthew 15:21-28

²¹ Leaving that place, Jesus withdrew to the region of Tyre and Sidon. ²² A Canaanite woman from that vicinity came to him, crying out, "Lord, Son of David, have mercy on me! My daughter is demon-possessed and suffering terribly." ²³ Jesus did not answer a word. So, his disciples came to him and urged him, "Send her away, for she keeps crying out after us." ²⁴ He answered, "I was sent only to the lost sheep of Israel." ²⁵ The woman came and knelt before him. "Lord, help me!" she said. ²⁶ He replied, "It is not right to take the children's bread and toss it to the dogs." ²⁷ "Yes, it is, Lord," she said. "Even the dogs eat the crumbs that fall from their master's table." ²⁸ Then Jesus said to her, "Woman, you have great faith! Your request is granted." And her daughter was healed at that moment."

SCRIPTURAL REVELATION: Jesus, how rude!!! This scriptural story can really make a parent angry, especially when your child is suffering, and the one person that can deliver that child is seemingly putting you off. Jesus' behavior must first be understood and put it in the correct context.

First, before this time, Jesus was always in the Jewish territory spreading the Good News of the Kingdom, and he mandated the disciples to do the same only in the Jewish territory, per the Father's instruction. (Matthew 10:6).

Second, Jesus is now in Gentile territory where he was withdrawing for a break or a chance to teach the disciples when this Canaanite (Gentile) woman comes up to him pleading for help.

Third, Gentiles were commonly referred to as 'dogs' by the Jewish community. Jews and Gentiles did not care for or get along with others. This statement was not to say that Jesus hated her, but this was custom at that time.

Fourth, while in Jewish territory, Jesus did heal Gentiles that have converted to the faith. So, it was not a matter that Jesus did not want to help her.

Now, looking even further, the disciples requested that Jesus send the woman away. However, Jesus never told her to leave his presence. He attempted to discourage her by telling her, not right now, I must first fulfill my mission to the Jews, and then I will help all others. Yet, this woman did a few things to get her daughter delivered: 1) She recognized Jesus as Lord, Son of David. 2) With this recognition, she had some knowledge of who Jesus was and his overall mission - to save the world (this includes everybody), so she refused his rebuke. 3) She refused to give up on getting the help her daughter needed. She was not told by the Lord to go away, to leave him alone, or even no. So, she kept on until she got what she wanted. In the end, her faith in knowing God's son's real heart, Jesus was to save the world, which included her (can you imagine living with a demon and the havoc it wreaked in the home?) and her daughter. This woman was desperate, and she spoke up for her daughter and herself for some peace.

REFLECTION: There were times, I spoke up and times in which I relied on God's provision. You choose the battle in everything in life. It was more important to me to have the respect of the doctors and other health care providers. Informing them of what will be accepted and not accepted. Having my daughter on several medications was not and is not an option. Understand, medication is sometimes needed to help balance, but I passionately believe that this society over-medicate our children. This is noted in all of her health records. So, whoever picks the file up, knows that prescribing medications is not the first thing that should be discussed. To this day, thank God she is on only one medication to help with anxiety and aggressiveness, and it is at the lowest dose possible with the ability to give her more if we, her mother and father, decide she needs more. She has remained on the same dosage, maybe a little higher since she started taking medication at age 16. (Yep, the hormones kicked in.)

Thankfully, our daughter had not needed to go to the doctor except for well-checkups until most recently when she started having stomach issues. We learned she was severely constipated. She could not keep anything down, and nothing on the other end was coming out. The doctor's first answer to solving the problem was to give her a big jug of MiraLax. I asked, 'How do you want me to do that? She is not keeping anything down. What good will that do?' The response, 'Oh! I see the problem.' I then asked curiously, 'outside of the textbook, what can we do?' During this time trying to figure out the most sensible plan, we also learned her iron was low (probably because she was not keeping food down). The doctor then wanted to prescribe her iron pills - I again asked, 'Doesn't iron cause constipation?' The doctor's response was, 'Yes, but if it causes her to be more constipated, we can prescribe her another pill to help with that?' Of course, I had the 'devil is a liar' look on my face. I politely stated, 'We are not going that route; let us get her current situation taken care of first. We are NOT going to give her medication and then give her another medication to counteract the other medication.' We ended up coming up with an alternative that worked after a few tries. Our daughter was able to regain her appetite and slowly but surely able to keep food down. Once the issue was resolved, we did not need the iron pills and no other long-term required medications. At the follow-ups, the doctor was amazed that she was doing so well.

If we had simply followed the textbook and 'this is how we treat everybody,' she would more than likely be on several medications that counteract each other. Just like the woman rebutted Jesus' textbook answer to her, you too have the authority and right to refute the textbook answers the healthcare professionals may try to give to you, or even any professional, school, therapists, church leaders for that matter.

MEDITATE AND ACTIVATE

ACKNOWLEDGE: You have not because you asked not, speak up. Do not worry about what someone thinks of you, especially when what you ask for is rightfully yours.

Matthew 7:7-8 *Ask, and it will be given to you; seek and you will find; knock and the door will be opened to you. For everyone who asks receives; the one who seeks finds; and to the one who knocks, the door will be opened.*

BELIEVE: You and your family are heirs to the Kingdom of God. You possess the key to unlock and open every locked and closed door.

Romans 8:17 *Now if we are children, then we are heirs—heirs of God and co-heirs with Christ, if indeed we share in his sufferings in order that we may also share in his glory.*

79

CONQUER:

1. Do not let anyone discourage you.

Psalm 55:22 *Cast your cares on the Lord and he will sustain you; he will never let the righteous be shaken.*

2. Do not let what others say about you keep you from getting what is rightfully yours. You do not have to accept this what we do for everyone else answer. You are unique, and your child is unique.

Romans 12:2 *Do not conform to the pattern of this world, but be transformed by the renewing of your mind.*

3. Remember, you have the right to request what you should have for yourself and your family.

Luke 11:9,10 *So, I say to you: Ask and it will be given to you; seek and you will find; knock and the door will be opened to you. ¹⁰For everyone who asks receives; the one who seeks finds; and to the one who knocks, the door will be opened.*

4. Be humbly persistent and God will provide. Ask questions. Get understanding.

Proverbs 4:7 *The beginning of wisdom is this: Get wisdom. Though it cost all you have, get understanding.*

ENCOURAGING WORD:

Choose your battles and, in those battles, rebut the system, not just for your child, but for the things you rightly deserve, including your PEACE OF MIND.

PRAYER

Dear Heavenly Father,
give me the words to say, the questions to ask, and the grace to say the things I need to say and ask for myself and for my loved one. Help me to advocate for myself and my loved one that is pleasing to you. Download your wisdom in me to know when to fight and when to rely on you. Thank you for being my advocate.
In Jesus' name,
Amen.

13

Ram in the Bush

SCRIPTURE: Genesis 22: 9-14

When they reached the place God had told him about, Abraham built an altar there and arranged the wood on it. He bound his son Isaac and laid him on the altar, on top of the wood. [10] Then he reached out his hand and took the knife to slay his son. [11] But the angel of the LORD called out to him from heaven, "Abraham! Abraham!" "Here I am," he replied. [12] "Do not lay a hand on the boy," he said. "Do not do anything to him. Now I know that you fear God, because you have not withheld from me your son, your only son." [13] Abraham looked up and there in a thicket he saw a ram caught by its horns. He went over and took the ram and sacrificed it as a burnt offering instead of his son. [14] So Abraham called that place The LORD Will Provide. And to this day it is said, "On the mountain of the LORD it will be provided."

SCRIPTURAL REVELATION: When looking at the story of Abraham and Isaac, Abraham was given probably one of the most challenging tasks - kill the child that was promised to him by God. Yet, the story shows Abraham's faith in God, knowing the power of God; Abraham probably knew that God made life, so He could also bring life back. As Abraham was about to slaughter his child, God stopped Him and showed a better sacrifice. God provided a 'Ram in the Bush.' God will always provide, even if it is at the last minute.

REFLECTION: As parents/caretakers of people with extraordinary needs, there are so many sacrifices we have to make. I often wonder if the sacrifice made is the right one, whether that sacrifice is made for the child or a personal sacrifice. At one point, every sacrifice came with a second guess. It took me some time to realize that I have to do what is right for my family and me. Either I completely trust God, or I do not. Finding good care for our daughter has always been a struggle; yet, I have always been willing to sacrifice to make sure she has loving care. One year, about three weeks before summer started, I thought I had daycare set up for my daughter. However, three weeks before school was to be released, when I called to confirm and talk some things over with the provider, she informed me she could not keep our daughter for the summer. She was doing something different for the summer. I thought she meant not keeping kids, but I later learned she still kept them, just not my daughter. Yes, I was heartbroken, devastated and now scrambling to figure out how I was going to maintain my job and care for her too. I cried and prayed. I decided that making sure she had appropriate care was a priority, and I was ready to be released from my job if that is what it takes. I contacted my manager and told her what happened, that I will need to take some time off to try to get something viable in place. She said she understood and to take the time I needed. I was relieved at her understanding and encouragement. A few days later, she called me back. She explained that she talked to the other people in our office about my situation, and they decided to take my workload for the summer so I could care for my daughter. I was speechless and in awe. To this day, I am so forever grateful for my work family doing this for me. That summer, in this particular instance, God provided several **'rams in the bush.'**

MEDITATE AND ACTIVATE

ACKNOWLEDGE: Sacrifices will be made and acknowledge that having faith and obedience to God is even more critical.

Hebrews 11:6 *Without faith, it is impossible to please God.*

I Samuel 15:22 *Obedience is better than sacrifice.*

BELIEVE: That with your faith and obedience, God will always provide. Sometimes the things that you are going through is to build your confidence and trust in God. He is always there, and He will always provide what you need. Take a moment to read **Psalms 23** (provided after Encouraging Word) and reflect on the Shepherd providing a place of rest, a place of refuge, protection from the enemy, provision, guidance, comfort when in the valley.

CONQUER:
1. Just as Abraham, trust God and be ready for the sacrifice. Trust and have faith in God. Abraham knew that God would provide a lamb for a sacrifice. He trusted God enough to know that the God he served did not use children as a sacrificial offering. In response to Isaac's question concerning a sacrifice when going up the mountain, Abraham responded that God will provide the lamb. Genesis 22:8

   Psalm 62:8 Trust in him at all times, you people; pour out your hearts to him, for God is our refuge.

2. No matter how hard it gets, keep the faith, keep going.

   Proverbs 3:5-6 *Trust in the Lord with all your heart and*

84

lean not on your own understanding; in all your ways submit to him, and he will make your paths straight.

3. Look up and expect God to provide.

Ephesians 3:20-21 *Now to him who is able to do immeasurably more than all we ask or imagine, according to his power that is at work within us, to him be glory in the church and in Christ Jesus throughout all generations, forever and ever! Amen.*

ENCOURAGING WORD:

'God always has something for you; a key for every problem, a light for every shadow, a relief for every sorrow and a plan for every tomorrow.' Author unknown.

Psalm 23

The LORD is my shepherd, I lack nothing.
 2 He makes me lie down in green pastures,
he leads me beside quiet waters,
 3 he refreshes my soul.
He guides me along the right paths
for his name's sake.
 4 Even though I walk
through the darkest valley,
I will fear no evil,
for you are with me;
your rod and your staff,
they comfort me.
 5 You prepare a table before me
in the presence of my enemies.
You anoint my head with oil;
my cup overflows.

⁶ Surely your goodness and love will follow me
all the days of my life,
and I will dwell in the house of the LORD
forever.

PRAYER

Dear Heavenly Father increase my faith
in you. Please help me to be obedient to
your Word and to your way even when I
do not understand. Thank you for your
provision and for always having a 'ram in
the bush.'
In Jesus' name, I pray,
Amen.

14

JESUS KNOWS AND SEES YOU:

Stay Persistent!

SCRIPTURE: John 5:5-8 (NKJV)

Now a certain man was there who had an infirmity thirty-eight years. When Jesus saw him lying there, and knew that he had already been in that condition a long time, He said to him, 'Do you want to be made well?' The sick man answered Him, 'Sir, I have no man to put me into the pool when the water is stirred up; but while I am coming, another steps down before me.' Jesus said to Him, 'Rise, take up your bed and walk.' And immediately the man was made well, took up his bed, and walked.

SCRIPTURAL REVELATION: During the feast of Jews, an angel will come and stir up the waters at a pool at the Sheep Gate. The pool is referred to as Bethesda. Many sick people with various disabilities would lay at this pool, waiting on the angel to stir the pool. Whoever was the first to get into the pool would be healed of their infirmities. At this pool, an unnamed man had been there for 38 years. When Jesus came by, He saw the man and knew he had been trying for a while. Jesus asked the man if he wanted to be healed. The man in a roundabout way said yes, but every time he tried, someone would jump in front of him. Hearing this, Jesus told the man to get up and take his bed and walk. The man did exactly that.

While many focus on the healing miracle at the pool in Bethesda, this lesson focuses on what Jesus sees. Jesus knows what you are going through, your troubles, as well as your persistence. So, do not give up!!!

REFLECTION: At times, it may seem your efforts are in vain. You think you finally figured it out, only to be -smack dab in the middle of another setback. Think about the man at the pool in Bethesda. He could not walk but somehow got right to the edge of the pool. He had it figured out, but then every time the water was stirred, he suffered a setback - someone more agile would jump ahead of him.

Jesus knowing and seeing this, offered him a way out by asking him if he wanted to be healed. The man, in his own way, accepted the offer and was instantly healed. The crazy thing is it took this man 38 years, but he did not give up. Because he did not give up, Jesus was there to help him out of his situation.

Even when it seems we cannot get ahead, know that He sees us, and He knows what we are going through. We may have to wait and try various treatments, medications, doctors, methods; but Jesus knows and sees exactly what we need. Just as the man at the pool had to accept the invitation, we need to accept the invitation knowing that He sees and knows. We must believe that he cares for us and is right there. When we accept and believe in these things, that sets us up to keep persisting and never giving up. Let Jesus be the wind beneath your wings.

ACKNOWLEDGE:
1. Jesus sees and knows what you are experiencing. He is your comforter.

Psalm 23:4 (NLT) *Even though I walk through the darkest valley, I will fear no evil, for you are with me; your rod and your staff, they comfort me.*

2. Just as Jesus knew what the man at the pool needed, he knows what each of us needs. We have to accept that his ways are not our ways and his thoughts are higher than our thoughts.

Isaiah 55:8-9 *For my thoughts are not your thoughts, neither are your ways my ways," declares the LORD. As the heavens are higher than the earth, so are my ways higher than your ways and my thoughts than your thoughts.*

BELIEVE:
1. Jesus is there, He cares and He will not leave nor forsake you.

Deuteronomy 31:8 - *The LORD himself goes before you and will be with you; he will never leave you nor forsake you. Do not be afraid; do not be discouraged.*

2. Just as Joshua was being sent into a strange land, God has appointed you to tackle different challenges. Moses reminds Joshua that God is always there. You should also be reminded that God is there - Do not be afraid or discouraged by the challenges ahead of you.

Joshua 1:*9 Have I not commanded you? Be strong and courageous. Do not be afraid; do not be discouraged, for the Lord your God will be with you wherever you go.*

3. God knows exactly what He is doing. He knows every hair on your head, he knows when you get up and lay down, He knows His plans for you!!! HE SEES and HE KNOWS!

Luke 12:6-7 *Are not five sparrows sold for two copper coins? And not one of them is forgotten before God. But the very hairs of your head are all numbered.*

Do not fear therefore; you are of more value than many sparrows.

Psalm 139:1-4 *You have searched me, Lord, and you know me. You know when I sit and when I rise; you perceive my thoughts from afar. You discern my going out and my lying down; you are familiar with all my ways. Before a word is on my tongue you, Lord, know it completely.*

Jeremiah 29:11 (MSG) *This is God's Word on the subject: "As soon as Babylon's seventy years are up and not a day before, I'll show up and take care of you as I promised and bring you back home. I know what I'm doing. I have it all planned out—plans to take care of you, not abandon you, plans to give you the future you hope for."*

CONQUER

1. When you feel hopeless and just about to give up, take captivity of your thoughts. If you do not, take captive of your thoughts, this hopelessness can become your feelings. Casting away thoughts of defeat, doubt, fear, and loneliness will help you break down strongholds

   II Corinthians 10:5 *We demolish arguments and every pretension that sets itself up against the knowledge of God, and we take captive every thought to make it obedient to Christ.*

2. Wait patiently for the Lord

   Psalm 40:1-3 *I waited patiently for the Lord's help; then he listened to me and heard my cry. He pulled me out of a dangerous pit, out of the deadly quicksand. He set me safely on a rock and made me secure. He taught me to sing a new song, a song of praise to our God. Many who see this will take warning and will put their trust in the Lord.*

3. Be strong and courageous for anything you have to face, no matter how great it may seem. If it does not happen immediately, that is okay. Listen to God; He has already made out the plans; follow His plans. Think about when young Solomon was handed the kingdom from his father, David. Solomon had a great job given to him by his father, David. God already knew and told David that he was not going to build the temple. God went on to tell David that his son Solomon would have that magnificent task. David had the plans God gave for the building of the temple. He encouraged Solomon not to be afraid or discouraged when seeing the great works, the Lord has for him but remembering that God loves you and will not forsake you in completing this task.

I Chronicles 28:20 *David also said to Solomon his son, "Be strong and courageous, and do the work. Do not be afraid or discouraged, for the Lord God, my God, is with you. He will not fail you or forsake you until all the work for the service of the temple of the Lord is finished.*

ENCOURAGING WORD:

When it seems you cannot get to the final destination and there is always something or someone that jumps in front of you; or, the task is so great you think you cannot do it and it will not get done. Remember that God sees you. He knows and has already planned it out; it is already taken care of. All you have to do is be willing to follow the blueprint - TRUST JESUS, GET UP, ACCEPT THE CHALLENGE, AND MOVE FORWARD!

PRAYER

Dear Heavenly Father, the blueprints are already made out. Please help me to trust you more and to know that you have already prepared a plan for my life that is prosperous, hopeful, and will not harm me. That through this trust, I will be obedient, and I will follow your steps, your plans, not my will Lord, but your will be carried out. Your will is that I can get to the finish line, that I can be healed, that I can do whatever you tasked me to do, and I conquer whatever challenge is set before me. I know I can do these things because you said so in your Word. Because you said so and because Lord, you planned it, I will not give up.
In Jesus' Name, I pray,
Amen.

15

IT'S NOT YOUR FAULT:

To God Be the Glory

SCRIPTURE: John 9:1-3

As he went along, he saw a man blind from birth. ² His disciples asked him, "Rabbi, who sinned, this man or his parents, that he was born blind?" ³ "Neither this man nor his parents sinned," said Jesus, "but this happened so that the works of God might be displayed in him.

SCRIPTURAL REVELATION: As Jesus was walking, he saw a blind man. Everyone knew this man was born blind. During biblical times (and perhaps still today in our culture), it was thought that if you had a disability or infirmity, it was caused by sin. Because the man was born blind and with preconceived ideas of sin, the disciples asked Jesus who was at fault - the baby born blind or the parents. At this point, Jesus changed the focus from placing blame to focusing on the fulfillment of purpose and answered that neither was at fault, but he was born blind so that God can get the Glory.

REFLECTION: How many times have you said if I had done this differently; or if I had not done that? I thought that the decisions I made about my body caused my child to be born with a disability. I thought that maybe if I had not gone on a trip to Georgia or ate that bag of pork rinds, my child would not have been born two months early. Or perhaps if I had taken better care of myself. The blame and guilt could go on and on. I do not know why nature took the course it did, but what I do know is that I am not God. I know that in life, there are going to be unexplainable happenings. I also know that when I stopped blaming myself and began focusing on God's purpose, and fulfillment, my and my daughter's life began to change drastically. I have gone from not getting my child into the church's doors to now her loving church, sitting in the sanctuary for service, and her not wanting to leave. When I shifted my focus, we have gone from not being able to go to the store to shop to going grocery or clothes shopping together. When I turned my focus, we went from her, not responding verbally to her vocalizing more and more. When I shifted my focus, we went from her waking us up every 2-3 hours at night to me now having to wake her up so she will not miss the bus.

MEDITATE AND ACTIVATE

ACKNOWLEDGE: We may not understand the cause, why, or how; however, you must realize that God's ways are not our ways and His thoughts are not our thoughts; and that his ways and thoughts are higher than ours.

Isaiah 55:8-9 *"For my thoughts are not your thoughts, neither are your ways my ways," declares the Lord. "As the heavens are higher than the earth, so are my ways higher than your ways and my thoughts than your thoughts."*

Nature has taken its course. You had no control over it. Some things happen that are out of our control.

BELIEVE: Believe your life has a purpose. God knows every detail of your life and your child's life. He knows your purpose and your child's purpose. When we begin to believe that God is in control, that God knows what He is doing, then He can start to operate in us to bring forth His purpose.

Jeremiah 29:11, *"For I know the plans I have for you,"* declares the LORD, *"plans to prosper you and not to harm you, plans to give you hope and a future."*

CONQUER:

1. Shift your focus - rather than looking at the cause or playing the blame game; ask God how you can use the challenges to give Him the Glory.

   I Corinthians 10:31 *So whether you eat or drink or whatever you do, do it all for the Glory of God.*

2. Stop taking credit and blaming yourself for something you could not have prevented. Trust God and Give Him the Glory.

   Proverbs 3:5-6 *Trust in the Lord with all your heart and lean not on your own understanding; in all your ways submit to him, and he will make your paths straight.*

ENCOURAGING WORD:

If you focus on the problem, the problem will become your focus. If you focus on Jesus, He will show you the way, the truth, and the light.

PRAYER

Dear Heavenly Father, please help me understand the things I can change and the things I cannot. Please help me trust you all the more and shift my focus from seeing a challenge to giving you all the Glory because you are all-knowing and all-powerful God. Your ways and thoughts are above my ways and thoughts. I give it all to you, and I praise you for being the wise magnificent God you are.
In Jesus' name,
Amen.

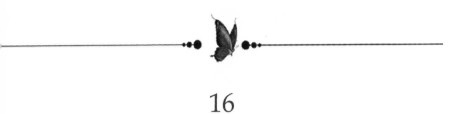

16

HAVE NO FEAR, YOU ARE NOT ALONE:

The Four Promises of God

SCRIPTURE: Isaiah 41:10
So do not fear, for I am with you; do not be dismayed, for I am your God. I will strengthen you and help you; I will uphold you with my righteous right hand.

SCRIPTURAL REVELATION: God, through His prophet Isaiah, is sending comfort to Israel, who was in distress due to their captivity in Babylon. Although in despair, God wanted to calm Israel's fears and encourage His people. God's promises given in this scripture still applies to His people who are bound and in distress today.

REFLECTION: Sometimes, I felt like I was not going to make it, especially in the early years. I felt like I had nobody; I was alone except I have this child that seemed to be out of control. I am just getting home from work; her bus pulls up, gets off, and goes into a total meltdown. She is pulling, scratching, screaming, refusing to walk down the driveway to go to the house. Dad is working a double shift; he will not be home until tomorrow morning. What am I to do? Help, somebody?

After about 45 minutes, I finally got her into the house. We dance a little to her favorite tunes; of course, I am tired, but trying to stay upbeat. She eats, and now it is time for bed. Here we go again. Going to bed for her was out of the question. I am on my last leg and ready for some relaxation; she wants to stay up. On top of that, if I sat down, she goes into a full-blown tantrum, pulling, scratching, screaming. I am so tired; please help? At this point, I am so tired I secured the cabinets and refrigerator in the kitchen, made sure everything was put up and went to my room and locked the door, fell on the floor, and cried. Yes, she was still up, but I had enough. She stood on the other end of the door, banging on the door. I thought, as long as she was doing this, I knew what she was doing. I never felt so alone in my life. I cried out to God; I cannot do this. I need relief. Help Lord!

I began talking to God- you gave her to me; you need to help me. You said you would never leave or forsake me, where are you? Your name is Emmanuel – that means God is with us, right? It was then God said you were never alone; I was right there with you. I was waiting for you to ask ME for help. Then I decided, ok God, what should I do? Join her, stop stressing; she is picking up on it and reacting to your distress. So, I went out of the room, yes, she was still in full mode. But I turned on her favorite music, we danced a little, and I cleaned a little. When I stopped stressing and worrying over her going to bed, while I was cleaning, she on her own laid on the sofa and went to sleep. Ok? Really? Is that how that works? I put some covers over her, kissed her good night, and went to bed.

Thinking about the conversation between God and me, I decided to put that to work once she got off the bus. Rather than stressing about it, whatever happens, happens. She gets home, gets off the bus, and refused to come into the house again. This time, I sat down with her in the middle of the driveway and said, when you are ready, I'm ready. I am not in a hurry. She screamed and pulled some, but eventually, she held her hand out, and we got up and walked down the driveway and into the house. After a while of doing this, she began to look forward to coming into the house. She knew a snack, and her music would be waiting for her. Thank you, Lord Jesus!

MEDITATE AND ACTIVATE

ACKNOWLEDGE: Know that there will be hard times. Even when you feel alone or in distress, God is there. It is ok to cry, be frustrated, angry, just as long as you give it all to Him. He is there to comfort you, strengthen you, and guide you. Even when David was in the wilderness and running from King Saul, David reached out to God. He knew even in the wilderness, God was there.

II Corinthians 1:3a - *" Praise be to the God and Father of our Lord Jesus Christ, the Father of compassion and the God of all comfort, who comforts us in all our troubles, . . ."*

BELIEVE: The promises God gave to the Israelites are for you too! He gave them four promises in Isaiah 41:10:

1ˢᵗ promise: **Do not fear, I am with thee; do not be dismayed; I am your God.** Believe that you are specifically chosen to be on this extraordinary journey, and through the ups and downs, God is with you - so do not fear or be dismayed with challenges set before you.

Deuteronomy 31:6 *God will never leave you, nor forsake you.*

2ⁿᵈ promise: **I will strengthen you.**

One of my favorite verses when I was a teenager:

Isaiah 40:29-31 *He gives strength to the weary and increases the power of the weak. ³⁰Even youths grow tired and weary, and young men stumble and fall; ³¹but those who hope in the LORD will renew their strength. They will soar on wings like eagles; they will run and not grow weary, they will walk and not be faint.*

New Testament Scripture - Believe Philippians 4:13 *I can do all things through Christ, **who strengthens you.***

3rd promise: ... **I will help you.** While there will be tests and trials, God will help you through all of it. He will not allow the challenges in your life go past your limits.

I Corinthians 10:13 (MSG) *No test or temptation that comes your way is beyond the course of what others have had to face. All you need to remember is that God will never let you down; he'll never let you be pushed past your limit; he'll always be there to help you come through it.*

4th promise: **I will uphold you with my righteous right hand.** Miriam-Webster defines uphold as to give support to; to support against an opponent; to keep elevated; to lift up. Believe that God is using his mighty sacred right hand to hold you up. Whatever challenge or challenges you are going through, God promises to give you support against that challenge, to keep you lifted and elevated.

Psalm 20:6 *Now this I know: The Lord gives victory to his anointed. He answers him from his heavenly sanctuary with the victorious power of his right hand.*

CONQUER:
1. Pray, ask God for help, and His wisdom in dealing with the challenges set before you.

   Philippians 4:6-7 *Do not be anxious about anything, but in every situation, by prayer and petition, with thanksgiving, present your requests to God. And the peace of God, which transcends all understanding, will guard your hearts and your minds in Christ Jesus.*

2. Do not stress, become dismayed, or fear the challenges that lie ahead of you.

    II Timothy 1:7 *God has not given 'you' the Spirit of Fear, but of power, love and sound mind.*

    Exercise those three things daily and you will be able to conquer anything set before you.

ENCOURAGING WORD:

I read or heard somewhere – *God does not give us what we can handle; God helps us handle what we are given.*

This is worth re-stating: I Corinthians 10:13 - (MSG)
No test or temptation that comes your way is beyond the course of what others have had to face. All you need to remember is that God will never let you down; he'll never let you be pushed past your limit; He'll always be there to help you come through it.'

PRAYER

Dear Heavenly Father, I can always count you
to be there with me in my time of peace, and
in my time of trouble. When I am happy and
when I am sad. I thank you. Even when I feel
lonely, I know that I am not, for you are
always with me, and you have not left me.
Thank you for being a guide, a comforter, and
a good, good father.
In Jesus' Name,

17

DON'T GIVE UP!

There's Power in the Press & Wait!

SCRIPTURE: Luke 8:40-56

And it came to pass, that, when Jesus was returned, the people gladly received him: for they were all waiting for him. ⁴¹And, behold, there came a man named Jairus, and he was a ruler of the synagogue: and he fell down at Jesus' feet, and besought him that he would come into his house: ⁴²For he had one only daughter, about twelve years of age, and she lay a dying. But as he went the people thronged him. ⁴³And a woman having an issue of blood twelve years, which had spent all her living upon physicians, neither could be healed of any, ⁴⁴Came behind him, and touched the border of his garment: and immediately her issue of blood stanched. ⁴⁵And Jesus said, Who touched me? When all denied, Peter and they that were with him said, Master, the multitude throng thee and press thee, and sayest thou, Who touched me? ⁴⁶And Jesus said, Somebody hath touched me: for I perceive that virtue is gone out of me. ⁴⁷And when the woman saw that she was not hid, she came trembling, and falling down before him, she declared unto him before all the people for what cause she had touched him, and how she was healed immediately. ⁴⁸And he said unto her, Daughter, be of good comfort: thy faith hath made thee whole; go in peace. ⁴⁹While he yet spake, there cometh one from the ruler of the synagogue's house, saying to him, Thy daughter is dead; trouble not the Master. [50]*But when Jesus heard it, he answered him, saying, Fear not: believe only, and she shall be made whole.* [51]*And when he came into the house, he suffered no man to go in, save Peter, and James, and John, and the father and the mother of the maiden.* [52]*And all wept, and bewailed her: but he said, Weep not; she is not dead, but sleepeth.* [53]*And they laughed him to scorn, knowing that she was dead.* [54]*And he put them all out, and took her by the hand, and called, saying, Maid, arise.* [55]*And her spirit came again, and she arose straightway: and he commanded to give her meat.* [56]*And her parents were astonished: but he charged them that they should tell no man what was done.*

SCRIPTURAL REVELATION: Two things are going on here, but both give the same message. While many will focus on the child being brought back from the dead or the instantaneous healing of the woman with the issue of blood, the scriptures go far beyond the end, but the means to getting to the end is far more critical. These stories both bring about the message that one must: 1. Have faith; 2. Press on 3. Not give up on your wait. The first story talks of a dad, Jairus, advocating for his child. He presses through the crowd to ask Jesus to come and heal his daughter on her death bed. Jesus complies with the request only to be stopped by a woman in the crowd (I will talk about this woman later). During the wait for Jesus, Jairus' daughter died. When Jesus arrives at Jairus home, he tells Jairus and wife, do not be afraid, believe, and your daughter will be healed. The parents must have believed. Their daughter was restored to them.

Now, for the woman who caused the delay. This woman suffered from menstrual bleeding for 12 years. She was an outcast. It was illegal for her to worship in the synagogue or have normal relationships due to her issue of blood. She was considered unclean, and anyone who touched her would also be regarded as unclean. She spent all of her money on doctors, potions, and lotions. Despite it being against the law, she had faith that if she could touch Jesus' garment, she would be healed. She decided to press her way through the crowd and made a deliberate act of touching the hem of Jesus' robe. The revelation I received from this was: 1. More than likely, she was on the ground going through the crowd as she was trying to be unnoticed. If you recall, she was considered unclean; it was illegal for her to be amongst the crowd. And 2. This woman was probably weak from anemia as well, and it was easier for her to press through the crowd on the ground avoiding bodies and stares. Nonetheless, upon her act of faith, her press and touching His hem, the woman was instantly healed.

REFLECTION: My advocacy for my child over the years has been somewhat different from others. In no way do I knock how parents advocate for their children; you must choose what you believe is best for you. After so many disappointments in relying on agencies and men to help, I decided to place my faith in Jesus and allow him to give the wisdom and resources we needed to raise our daughter. Yes, she went to the doctors for her physical and diagnosis; but the community service was a great fail. In one instance, I went to the agency and applied for assistance. Unfortunately, despite my efforts to reach out, I did not receive a follow up letter, or a return phone call. I received nothing.

After about two years, a lady from the agency calls out of nowhere, stating she was cleaning up files and noticed services were not followed up with and wanted to know if we still wanted services. Even though it had been two years, I said yes and went to the office, updated information, and rescheduled an appointment with her to talk about services. I went back to the rescheduled appointment, and she looked at me as if I lost my mind and told me we did not have an appointment. After a few words (I was kind), I left, and I never heard from her again about anything. I was so disappointed. It was then; I decided that my advocacy would have to be something I do through God in making sure my daughter had what she needed. I sought Him and was able to get the services she required: afterschool care, therapy, etc. God provided our family with the necessary resources to get these things, along with the help of family and friends, we were able to make it through, even during the hard times. It was not always easy, but I was able to go a different route and press through to get what was needed. After those that were supposed to help failed, the woman with the issue of blood went a different route. Following her example, I put my faith in God, found a different route through the crowd, and pressed through to get to Jesus. Just as with Jairus, help may have been delayed, but not denied. My help comes from the Lord.

MEDITATE AND ACTIVATE

ACKNOWLEDGE:

1. That Jesus is our Lord and Savior, that through Him all things are possible-

   Luke 18:27. *"What is impossible to man is possible with God."*

2. There will, often be a deliberate press that is needed; there may also be a season where one must wait.

   Philippians 3:12-14 - *"Not that I have already obtained all this, or have already arrived at my goal, but I press on to take hold of that for which Christ Jesus took hold of me. Brothers and sisters, I do not consider myself yet to have taken hold of it. But one thing I do: Forgetting what is behind and straining toward what is ahead, I press on toward the goal to win the prize for which God has called me heavenward in Christ Jesus."*

3. That advocacy for you and your child may not be the same route as your neighbor or friend with an exceptional child. Your route through the crowd may be different, and that is okay. The important thing is that you get on your route, and you press through it.

   Isaiah 42:16 - *"I will lead the blind by ways they have not known, along unfamiliar paths I will guide them; I will turn the darkness into light before them and make the rough places smooth. These are the things I will do; I will not forsake them."*

BELIEVE:
1. You must have faith; that means believing in something before you see it happens.

   Hebrews 11:1 - *"Faith is the substance of things hoped for, evidence of things not seen."*

2. However, you decide to advocate, it will take some pressing and waiting, but that thing you hoped for will happen.

   Proverbs 13:12 - *"Hope deferred makes the heart sick, but a longing fulfilled is a tree of life."*

3. That you are important too! What is it that you believe God for? Do not let the crowd or circumstance stop you.

There is enough power to do both for you and your child. (This scripture has two stories in which Jesus exercised his power, he did not run out)

Matthew 10:29-31 - *"Are not two sparrows sold for a penny? Yet not one of them will fall to the ground outside your Father's care. And even the very hairs of your head are all numbered. So don't be afraid; you are worth more than many sparrows."*

CONQUER:

1. Do not give up, keep going, even if you cannot see through the crowd, keep pressing.

   James 1:2-4 - *"Consider it pure joy, my brothers and sisters, whenever you face trials of many kinds because you know that the testing of your faith produces perseverance. Let perseverance finish its work so that you may be mature and complete, not lacking anything."*

2. Learn what you can from others, seek God's wisdom, and implement it. It amazes me that this woman was not allowed to go to the synagogue or be in a crowd of people due to her condition, but she knew and learned enough about Jesus to know he can heal her.

   James 1:5-6 - *"If any of you lacks wisdom, you should ask God, who gives generously to all without finding fault, and it will be given to you. But when you ask, you must believe and not doubt, because the one who doubts is like a wave of the sea, blown and tossed by the wind."*

3. Be bold in your faith and press.

   Ephesians 3:11-12 -"*According to the eternal purpose which he purposed in Christ Jesus our Lord: In whom we have boldness and access with confidence by the faith of him.*"

4. Parents, even though the press and wait, add some time for yourself. It is not taboo to want to be restored (just as this woman with the issue of blood). We, too, need to have our strength renewed.

   God even rested (not because He was tired, but to enjoy the beauty of His creation)

   Genesis 2:2-3 (NLT) - "*On the seventh day God had finished his work of creation, so he rested from all his work. And God blessed the seventh day and declared it holy, because it was the day when he rested from all his work of creation.*"

   God encourages you to rest too:
   Psalm 23:2 (NLT) - "*He lets me rest in green meadows; he leads me beside peaceful streams. He renews my strength...*"

ENCOURAGING WORD:

Remember, your help comes from the Lord. Have Faith, Press, and Wait. You may think it is delayed, but it is not denied. He will always be on time.

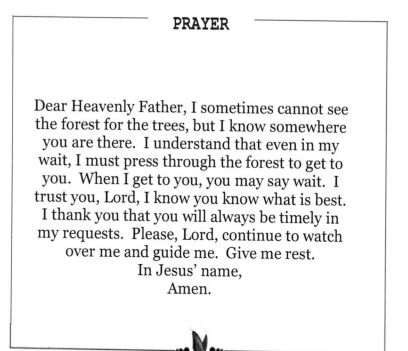

PRAYER

Dear Heavenly Father, I sometimes cannot see the forest for the trees, but I know somewhere you are there. I understand that even in my wait, I must press through the forest to get to you. When I get to you, you may say wait. I trust you, Lord, I know you know what is best. I thank you that you will always be timely in my requests. Please, Lord, continue to watch over me and guide me. Give me rest.
In Jesus' name,
Amen.

Built for This!

Encouraging Words

This last section was not even on my radar to do. Thanks to Empower Me Books for encouraging me to reflect on the different families that are out there. We sometimes take it for granted that one family has it easier than the other. It is simply not true. We all have our ups and downs. Whatever family type you have, remember – God is with you and to

Stay Encouraged!

We all have a race to run, whether individual or relay. The goal for both is to keep going and get to the finish line.

~ Dietrich

18

FOR THE MARRIED

Pass the Baton: This is a Relay Race

BUT IF YOU DROP THE BATON, PICK IT UP AND KEEP RUNNING

SCRIPTURE: Luke 2:41-52

⁴¹ Every year Jesus' parents went to Jerusalem for the Festival of the Passover. ⁴² When he was twelve years old, they went up to the festival, according to the custom. ⁴³ After the festival was over, while his parents were returning home, the boy Jesus stayed behind in Jerusalem, but they were unaware of it. ⁴⁴ Thinking he was in their company, they traveled on for a day. Then they began looking for him among their relatives and friends. ⁴⁵ When they did not find him, they went back to Jerusalem to look for him. ⁴⁶ After three days they found him in the temple courts, sitting among the teachers, listening to them and asking them questions. ⁴⁷ Everyone who heard him was amazed at his understanding and his answers. ⁴⁸ When his parents saw him, they were astonished. His mother said to him, "Son, why have you treated us like this? Your father and I have been anxiously searching for you." ⁴⁹ "Why were you searching for me?" he asked. "Didn't you know I had to be in my Father's house?" ⁵⁰ But they did not understand what he was saying to them. ⁵¹ Then he went down to Nazareth with them and was obedient to them. But his mother treasured all these things in her heart. ⁵² And Jesus grew in wisdom and stature, and in favor with God and man.

SCRIPTURAL REVELATION: Mary and Joseph lost the Savior. Can you believe it? How do you lose the sent One? Can you imagine, Joseph thought Jesus was with Mary. Mary thought Jesus was with Joseph. Until they asked each other, 'Where was the boy? Can you imagine how they must have felt losing their child? Their family did not know where he was, and eventually, Mary and Joseph had to backtrack to find him. Even the ones that God chose to birth and raise the Savior made mistakes. They dropped the ball.

REFLECTION: To lose a child is the worse feeling. Especially when your child does not understand and appreciate the danger. They see a chance to run and they run. I called our daughter an escape artist. She would figure out how to unlock the doors and leave. The last time she was gone for probably about 15 minutes before we realized she was gone. Her dad thought she was upstairs with me, and I thought she was downstairs with her dad. She had found a barely used backdoor, unlocked it, and went out. My heart sank. We searched and searched, finally finding her a couple of streets over. Some kind man stopped and assisted her to safety. Thank God she was safe and unharmed. She was still giggling, not knowing the danger she was or could have been in.

I just about fainted when she walked through the front door. Now, my husband and I are constantly checking in and communicating with each other. We also changed the locks and put sensors on each of the doors and windows. If I am upstairs and downstairs and hear a door open, I can either look on the camera or call downstairs to see if my husband is opening the door. Just like when Mary and Joseph lost Jesus, there will be times when we as parents will drop the ball. My husband and I did not blame each other but strengthened our bond and put things in place to make sure the baton of responsibility is firmly handed to the other person. Sometimes the baton is dropped; we are only human. The blame game is not helpful; we pick the baton back up, hold on tighter, and keep running.

MEDITATE AND ACTIVATE

ACKNOWLEDGE: You are in this together. Acknowledged that mistakes and oversights will happen. Then talk about it and figure out a game plan to make sure it does not happen again. Pick the baton up and keep on pressing forward and running in love. Do not let it tear you apart.

Ephesians 4:2-3 *Be completely humble and gentle; be patient, bearing with one another in love. Make every effort to keep the unity of the Spirit through the bond of peace.*

BELIEVE: Your marriage is strong, and let your love conquer the things that come before you.

1 Peter 4:8 *Above all, love each other deeply, because love covers over a multitude of sins.*

CONQUER:

1. Communicate, communicate, communicate. It is not just about the child, but how each other is feeling about your schedules and life – the good, bad, and ugly. Listen. Talk. Love.
2. Do not blame. Be understanding that we are human – mistakes, oversights will happen. Be there for each other.
3. Pray for each other.
4. Be flexible.
5. Be respectful of each other.
6. Give each other a break.
7. Find time to spend with each other. At least once a week. Get creative.

I Corinthians 13:4-7 *Love is patient, love is kind. It does not envy; it does not boast; it is not proud. It does not dishonor others; it is not self-seeking; it is not easily angered; it keeps no record of wrongs. Love does not delight in evil but rejoices with the truth. It always protects, always trusts, always hopes, always perseveres.*

ENCOURAGING WORD:

Marriage is hard enough. Now with the extra needs, it is even more of a blessing to the couple. You currently have reason to get closer, hold on even stronger, and love harder.

PRAYER

Dear Heavenly Father, you are the epitome of love. You are Love. We strive to love like you with forgiveness, understanding, and respect. Though we may have different navigation of this world, we take it on with pride. We do not forget each other's emotions or needs. We will keep you in the midst of our bond, and with you, in the midst, we cannot be broken.
In Jesus' Name,
Amen.

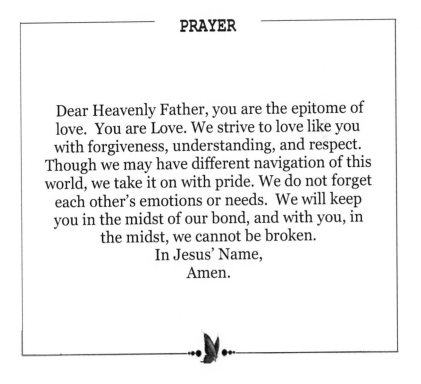

USE WHAT YOU GOT:

God Will Bless You with the Rest

SCRIPTURE: 2 Kings 4:4-7

4 *The wife of a man from the company of the prophets cried out to Elisha, "Your servant, my husband is dead, and you know that he revered the* LORD. *But now his creditor is coming to take my two boys as his slaves."* 2 *Elisha replied to her, "How can I help you? Tell me, what do you have in your house?" "Your servant has nothing there at all," she said, "except a small jar of olive oil."* 3 *Elisha said, "Go around and ask all your neighbors for empty jars. Don't ask for just a few.* 4 *Then go inside and shut the door behind you and your sons. Pour oil into all the jars, and as each is filled, put it to one side."* 5 *She left him and shut the door behind her and her sons. They brought the jars to her and she kept pouring.* 6 *When all the jars were full, she said to her son, "Bring me another one." But he replied, "There is not a jar left." Then the oil stopped flowing.* 7 *She went and told the man of God, and he said, "Go, sell the oil and pay your debts. You and your sons can live on what is left."*

SCRIPTURAL REVELATION: The widow was at her wit's end, bills were due, and the bill collectors were knocking on her door. She was about to lose everything, even her children. All she had was faith and olive oil. She knew the Lord because she stated her husband revered (or worshipped) the Lord; based on that, she had enough confidence to ask the man of God for help. When asked what she had, she said nothing, but olive oil and just a little bit of that. Based on her faith, she did what the man of God, the Prophet Elisha, told her to do. He told her to do three things:

1. Ask your neighbors and friends for help - 'ask all your neighbors for empty jars.'
2. Then go into a secret place - 'Go inside and shut the door behind you and your sons.'
3. Allow the anointing to flow - 'Pour oil into all the jars, and as each is filled, put it to one side.'

The widow did precisely as the Prophet told her to do. First, she relied on her neighbors to help her; she did not know why she had to ask for the jar. She could not tell them what they would be for, she just asked for them. This shows that those that are closest to you would not mind helping or giving you things that you request. No questions asked; they are always glad to help.

Second, go into your secret place. There are times God wants you to worship Him in secret. You do not have to place it on social media or announce what you are going through to the entire world. *Matthew 6:6-8* *⁶But when you pray, go into your room, close the door and pray to your unseen Father. Then your Father, who sees what is done in secret, will reward you. ⁷And when you pray, do not keep on babbling like pagans, for they think they will be heard because of their many words. ⁸Do not be like them, for your Father knows what you need before you ask him.*

Last, when you are in your secret place, worshipping God (following God's instructions is a form of worship), his anointing will flow. The widow's faith and obedience turned a little into enough to pay her debts and have some leftover to live.

REFLECTION: I have great admiration for the single parent, and one with a child or children with extra needs has my heart. Single parents caring for a loved one with special needs puts me in awe. Their strength, courage, and faith are unparalleled to anything I have seen or known. For instance, I have seen one parent with seven children, at least three who had different needs, go from homelessness to becoming a professional Real Estate Agent. Another parent having a child with autism had to flee an abusive home to start all over again in a new state. This parent started from the bottom and is now living in a stable home with the child. Both of these parents are amazing to me. I have been able to peek inside their window to see they were just like this widow. They were at their wit's end, at the end of their ropes, desperate. Yet, every time I talked with them, they had unparalleled faith that things would get better. That God would see them through. They have had to rely on close friends to help them get from one place to another; they went into a secret place where no one could see their prayers, their cries, and the obedience is given to the Lord. When they were weak, they did not blast on social media. They cried out to God and those they could trust around them. Many do not know half of their story. I am still learning, and I hope that one day they will share their testimony in full. How they started with little or nothing but used what they did have to go from being a victim to both being VICTORS with the anointing of God flowing so heavily on them. Their stories would make the average person ponder How They Got Over. These parents have Incredible strength, Incredible faith, and Incredible anointing, they used what they had, and God blessed them with the rest.

ACKNOWLEDGE: Nothing is too small for God to use and bless you. If your faith is small, use it and watch it grow. If all you have is a little, God can turn anything to be sufficient.

Matthew 17:20 *". . . Truly I tell you, if you have faith as small as a mustard seed, you can say to this mountain, 'Move from here to there,' and it will move. Nothing will be impossible for you."*

BELIEVE: That God will supply all of your needs.

Philippians 4:19 *And my God will meet all your needs according to the riches of his glory in Christ Jesus.*

CONQUER:
1. Follow the Word of God.

John 14:21 *Whoever has my commands and keeps them is the one who loves me. The one who loves me will be loved by my Father, and I too will love them and show myself to them.*

2. Do not be ashamed to ask for help from those that are trustworthy and you trust.

   Matthew 7:7-8 *Ask and it will be given to you; seek and you will find; knock and the door will be opened to you. For everyone who asks receives; the one who seeks finds; and to the one who knocks, the door will be opened.*

3. Some things should be for you and your family. Discern, who is there to help you and who is there to harm you.

   Proverbs 12:26 *The righteous choose their friends carefully, but the way of the wicked leads them astray.*

4. Understand that you must have faith and worship the Lord. This entails going into that secret place and following His instructions.

   Matthew 6:6 *But when you pray, go into your room, close the door and pray to your Father, who is unseen. Then your Father, who sees what is done in secret, will reward you.*

ENCOURAGING WORD:

Use what you got!!! Even when you feel as if you are raising your child alone, know that God has placed certain people in your life to help you and encourage you. Keep the faith, ask when you need, go into your secret place, and pray and worship the Lord. Just like oil, watch His anointing flow in your life.

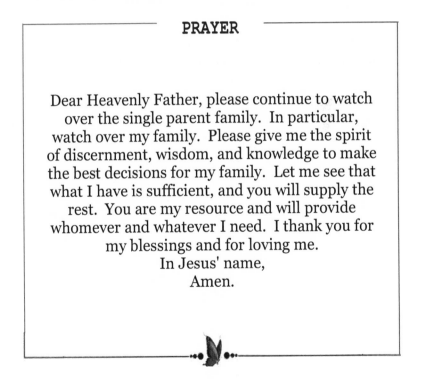

PRAYER

Dear Heavenly Father, please continue to watch over the single parent family. In particular, watch over my family. Please give me the spirit of discernment, wisdom, and knowledge to make the best decisions for my family. Let me see that what I have is sufficient, and you will supply the rest. You are my resource and will provide whomever and whatever I need. I thank you for my blessings and for loving me.
In Jesus' name,
Amen.

OFFER OF SALVATION

Knowing and experiencing the love of Jesus Christ is phenomenal. God does not expect perfection (even Jesus' parents messed up). We all have fallen short (Romans 3:23). Because of this, God has sent us His beloved Son, who came to save us and cover our sins. (John 3:16) Through Him, there are so many advantages - He came to give us life and life more abundantly (John 10:10) and peace that surpasses all understanding (Philippians 4:7), just to name a few. If you have not already accepted Jesus Christ as your Lord and Savior to access all He has to offer, you can accept Him today. Turn your heart and mind to Jesus by saying the following:

*"Jesus, I have done some things wrong that I genuinely am remorseful and grieved. I choose today to turn from those wrong things. I **A**cknowledge that I am in need of a savior and you are God's only son. I **B**elieve that You died for me. You were resurrected and you are the only true living Lord. I **C**onfess with my mouth these things, and with this confession, I have come unto Salvation. I am now an heir in the family of believers, and now I am saved."*

If you in your heart, said these things and meant it, WELCOME to the family. Understand that you will not be perfect. I am not perfect. No one is, but Jesus is a forgiving God; He loves you and extends to you grace and mercy. Thank you, Jesus!

Next Step - find a Bible-believing, teaching church in your area. If you have questions, please visit www.LifeDesignedbyGod.com and fill out the contact information, and someone on the team will get back to you. Congratulations, and remember to always

Stay Encouraged!!!

Love,

Dietrich McMillan
Life is Designed by God

AUTHOR BIO

Dietrich McMillan was born in Charlotte, North Carolina, to Charles and Deborah Dye. She is married to Antoine McMillan. They have two God sent children, Travis J. McMillan, and Brittney S. McMillan.

Dietrich, very early in her life, felt the call to serve God's people. She served in her childhood church in Charlotte as a youth usher, youth elder, and various other committees until she left to attend college. Dietrich attended North Carolina Central University undergraduate program. Then furthered her career and attended North Carolina Central University School of Law, where she received her Juris Doctorate. Dietrich passed the North Carolina State Bar exam in 1997 and began her service to the community as an Attorney.

Her heart and primary focus is has always been to help those disadvantaged financially and to encourage and uplift those that have been broken. She currently works with Legal Aid of North Carolina as a Domestic Violence Prevention Initiative Attorney helping domestic violence victims become victors.

In 2020, Dietrich received her Master's in Divinity and is pursuing her Doctorate in Theology. Dietrich believes that it is always important to build on your relationship with God, and it is essential to get as much knowledge as possible, both naturally and spiritually.

Dietrich is a member of One Love Christian Church under the Pastoral leadership of Pastor John C. Fitzpatrick, Jr., and Elder Pauline Fitzpatrick. She serves on several committees. Her heart and primary focus is serving the community through One Loves Outreach Team, Winning Souls to share the love of Jesus by fulfilling the needs of the people and ministering to them, according to Matthew 25:35-36 and Matthew 28:19-20.

Still feeling a higher calling to help others, Dietrich wanted to reach out to parents that have children or other family members that have extra/exceptional/special needs. Brittney was born two months early, two states away from home, and during the last year of Dietrich's law school career. Yet, through the strength of Jesus Christ, Dietrich was able to prevail, pass the bar and assist others on their journey.

Dietrich's greatest desire is to let every parent know they can accomplish whatever God has for them to do, and while the journey may be challenging, God is right

there with them every step of the way. To do this, Dietrich started a non-profit Designed by God, Inc. Designed by God is designed to let parents/caretakers know they are not alone and that they are loved by giving parents a different way of seeing through the lenses of God. For more information on the organization, Designed by God, Inc., visit the website LifeDesignedByGod.com

BOOK REVIEWS

"This was so amazing I really enjoyed reading your beginning. This really took me back when I first met you. I always knew you were a person I needed to get to know .I'm so proud to be able to call you my friend.
Thanking God for all he has showered you with so many gifts .
Keep up the great work."

-Midori Brooks-
Community Health Worker
Durham, NC

Thanks for reading! Please add a short review on Amazon.com and let me know what you thought!